D1596071

The Romantic Tradition
in American Literature

The Romantic Tradition in American Literature

Advisory Editor

HAROLD BLOOM
Professor of English, Yale University

THE

POEMS

OF

HENRY TIMROD

EDITED, WITH A SKETCH OF THE POET'S LIFE

BY

PAUL H. HAYNE

ARNO PRESS

A NEW YORK TIMES COMPANY

New York • 1972

Reprint Edition 1972 by Arno Press Inc.

Reprinted from a copy in The University
of Illinois Library

The Romantic Tradition in American Literature
ISBN for complete set: 0-405-04620-0
See last pages of this volume for titles.

Manufactured in the United States of America

ᏜᏜᏜᏜᏜᏜᏜᏜᏜᏜᏜ

Library of Congress Cataloging in Publication Data

Timrod, Henry, 1828-1867.
   The poems of Henry Timrod.

   (The Romantic tradition in American literature)
   I. Series.
PS3070.A2 1972   811'.3   72-4976
ISBN 0-405-04646-4

THE

POEMS

OF

HENRY TIMROD.

EDITED, WITH A SKETCH OF THE POET'S LIFE,

BY

PAUL H. HAYNE.

NEW YORK:

E. J. HALE & SON, PUBLISHERS,

MURRAY STREET.

1873.

LANGE, LITTLE & HILLMAN,
PRINTERS, ELECTROTYPERS AND STEREOTYPERS,
108 TO 114 WOOSTER STREET, N. Y.

TO THE

POET'S WIFE AND SISTER,*

AND TO HIS EARNEST FRIENDS, THE

HON. GEORGE S. BRYAN,

OF CHARLESTON, S. C.,

AND

DOCTOR J. DICKSON BRUNS,

OF NEW ORLEANS,

THIS VOLUME IS

𝔇𝔢𝔡𝔦𝔠𝔞𝔱𝔢𝔡.

---

* This Sister died soon after the "Dedication" was penned.

CONTENTS.

MEMOIR

OF

HENRY TIMROD.

THE name and writings of HENRY TIMROD have been long known and appreciated at the South. Nor are they wholly unknown at the North. I have before me a letter from the Quaker poet, WHITTIER, in which he warmly commends the poems of TIMROD he had seen, while expressing a regret for his early death.

Frequently, in his critical essays, RICHARD HENRY STODDARD has referred to TIMROD, as in his opinion the ablest poet the South had yet produced—a verdict fully sustained by some other (Northern) writers of high position, to whose notice the poems had been brought.

These facts may prove, in some sort, an introduction to the present volume, so far as the Northern public is concerned. They may win for it a candid examination, all that is necessary, doubtless, for its success.

Meanwhile, I purpose to give a sketch of TIMROD's life, which, though comparatively brief, and to an exceptional degree uneventful, is still of interest, as throwing much light upon the character of his verses, and the development of his genius.

HENRY TIMROD was born in Charleston, S. C., on the 8th
of December, 1829. He was the son of WILLIAM H. TIM-
ROD, whose father (HENRY TIMROD), a native of Germany,
had married Miss GRAHAM, a gifted and highly educated
lady of the north of Ireland, though of Scotch descent, and
in good, if not affluent, circumstances. Mr. TIMROD had
been for a considerable time a resident in this country, and
was, it seems, a widower, when Miss GRAHAM came to
Carolina. Sometime in 1792, their only son, WILLIAM, was
born on a plantation not far from Charleston.

Upon the death of his father, which occurred unfortu-
nately while the lad was quite young, his mother married
again; a step by which the family means, already reduced
by the exigencies of a revolutionary time, were still further
squandered.

Nevertheless, an effort was made by the mother to educate
her son for the Bar. It was frustrated in a manner at once
ludicrous and provoking. At the age of eleven, WILLIAM,
then at school, became possessed of an *idea*—a brilliant,
fascinating conception—which he must seize the first opportunity of practically testing. To the boy's fancy the most
enviable of mortals appeared to be, not a king or a conquer-
ing soldier, but a *bookbinder !*

Reasoning from his narrow premises, he concluded that
this lucky craftsman must, by the necessities of his position,
have access to innumerable volumes, and to stores of untold
learning. In order to realize this personally, and to live
thenceforth in a beatified atmosphere of Russia leather, he
ran away from school, and having found his Phœnix—a
complacent bookbinder—placed himself deliberately under
his tuition. Of course the intelligent lad must soon have
perceived how his dreams of the trade and its æsthetic
facilities had deceived him; but whether actuated by self-

will, or some better motive not revealed to others, he resisted both his mother's entreaties and the remonstrances of friends, refusing utterly to return to his orthodox studies.

Thus, by his own erratic will, the father of the poet became a mechanic—a skilled mechanic, we have been told—and rather proud than otherwise, like the true man he was, of his useful and honest craft.*

In the course of time, WILLIAM TIMROD, self-educated, but full of information, especially in English *belles lettres*, attracted the attention of his fellow-citizens by his brilliant talents. The wise and the gifted were happy to associate with him; and by the simple mastery of genius, he gained no trifling influence among the highest intellectual and social circles of a city noted at that period for aristocratic exclusiveness. Lawyers, politicians, editors, *littérateurs*, and gentlemen of scholarly ease and culture, would gather about his place of work, chiefly for the delight of listening to his unpremeditated and eloquent conversation. He seems indeed to have been—*longo intervallo*—a provincial Coleridge, holding his little audiences spell-bound by the mingled audacity and originality of his remarks.

Nor were his gifts exclusively conversational. On the contrary, that he possessed the special endowments of a poet, and of a poet of no mean order, some of the songs and sonnets he has left us clearly demonstrate.

---

* When the young aspirant after knowledge became bound to his master, he found that he had neither much time given him in the day to read, nor light at night!—"I have heard him declare," says one of his daughters, "that he used, when the moon was clear, or at its full, to climb on the leads of the house, and there, by the lunar rays, to read into the small hours of the night: Shakspeare was, at that time, his favorite companion."

Of these, an Ode "To Time,"* an apostrophe to "The Mocking Bird," and a *Sonnet* called "*Autumnal Day in Carolina,*" are the most finished and striking. I will quote them here.

TO TIME—THE OLD TRAVELLER.

I.

" They slander thee, Old Traveller,
    Who say that thy delight
Is to scatter ruin, far and wide,
    In thy wantonness of might :
For not a leaf that falleth
    Before thy restless wings,
But in thy flight, thou changest it
    To a thousand brighter things.

II.

" Thou passest o'er the battle-field
    Where the dead lie stiff and stark,
Where naught is heard save the vulture's scream,
    And the gaunt wolf's famished bark ;
But thou hast caused the grain to spring
    From the blood-enrichéd clay,
And the waving corn-tops seem to dance
    To the rustic's merry lay.

---

* These *four* stanzas, " To Time," formed a portion, originally, of a much longer poem. Oddly enough, they occur in a very unambitious production, viz., a newspaper " *Carrier's Address.*"

Apropos of the verses, Judge Bryan, in a private letter to me, observes,

" As one proof of the excellence of the ode, " *To Time,*" let me say here what it would have delighted me to have said to the author, that on my reciting this poem to Washington Irving, he exclaimed with fervor, that ' Tom Moore had written no finer lyric.' "

III.

" Thou hast strewed the lordly palace
        In ruins o'er the ground,
    And the dismal screech of the owl is heard
        Where the harp was, wont to sound ;
    But the self-same spot thou coverest
        With the dwellings of the poor,
    And a thousand happy hearts enjoy
        What *one* usurped before!

IV.

" 'Tis true thy progress layeth
        Full many a loved one low,
    And for the brave and beautiful
        Thou hast caused our tears to flow ;
    But always near the couch of death
        Nor thou, nor we can stay,
    And the breath of thy departing wings,
        Dries all our tears away!"
    *   *   *   *   *   *   *   *

THE MOCKING BIRD.

" Nor did lack
Sweet music to the magic of the scene :
The little crimson-breasted Nonpareil
Was there, his tiny feet scarce bending down
The silken tendril that he lighted on
To pour his love-notes—and in russet coat,
Most homely, like true genius bursting forth
In spite of adverse fortune—a full choir
Within himself—the merry Mock Bird sate,
Filling the air with melody—and at times,
In the rapt fervor of his sweetest song,

His quivering form would spring into the sky,
In spiral circles, as if he would catch
New powers from kindred warblers in the clouds,
Who would bend down to greet him ! "
*   *   *   *   *   *   *   *

AUTUMNAL DAY IN CAROLINA.

A SONNET.

" Sleeps the soft South, nursing its delicate breath
   To fan the first buds of the early spring,
And summer sighing, mourns his faded wreath,
   Its many-colored glories withering
Beneath the kisses of the new-waked North,
   Who yet in storms approaches not—but smiles
On the departing season, and breathes forth
   A fragrance, as of summer—till at whiles,
All that is sweetest in the varying year,
   Seems softly blent in one delicious hour,
Waking dim visions of some former sphere,
   Where sorrows—such as earth owns—had no power
To veil the changeless lustre of the skies,
And mind and matter formed one Paradise ! "
*   *   *   *   *   *   *   *

Not equal in poetical merit to the foregoing, but even
more interesting because of their subject, are the lines which
follow.   They are mournfully prophetic:

TO HARRY.

" Harry, my little blue-eyed boy,
   I love to hear thee playing near ;
There's music in thy shouts of joy
   To a fond father's ear.

" I love to see the lines of mirth
    Mantle thy cheek and forehead fair,
  As if all pleasures of the earth
    Had met to revel there ;

" For gazing on thee, do I sigh
    That these most happy hours will flee,
  And thy full share of misery
    Must fall in life on thee !

" There is no lasting grief below,
    My Harry ! that flows not from guilt ;
  Thou can'st not read my meaning now—
    In after times thou wilt.

" Thou'lt read it when the churchyard clay
    Shall lie upon thy father's breast,
  And he, though dead, will point the way
    Thou shalt be always blest.

" They'll tell thee this terrestrial ball,
    To man for his enjoyment given,
  Is but a state of sinful thrall
    To keep the soul from heaven.

" My boy ! the verdure-crowned hills,
    The vales where flowers innumerous blow,
  The music of ten thousand rills
    Will tell thee, 'tis not so.

" God is no tyrant who would spread
    Unnumbered dainties to the eyes,
  Yet teach the hungering child to dread
    That touching them he dies !

> " No ! all can do his creatures good,
>   He scatters round with hand profuse—
> The only precept understood,
>   ' *Enjoy, but not abuse !* ' "

In the Nullification controversy of 1832–3, when all South
Carolina was convulsed as with the throes of a political and
moral earthquake, when, in Charleston especially, a bitterness of party feeling prevailed, which threatened at any
moment to precipitate revolution and bloodshed, WILLIAM
TIMROD espoused the cause of ·the *Union* with all the ardor
and enthusiasm of his poet soul.

One morning, while at work in his employer's store, the
" *divine afflatus* " came suddenly upon him, and he composed
the following fiery song, which, doubtless, has the true
lyric ring, although, as might have been anticipated under
the circumstances, it does grave injustice to the motives and
character of the leaders of Nullification. In the midst of
composing these verses, he became, we are told, "so trans-
ported with the passion of his work," that rushing from his
own small room in the rear, he fairly *shouted out* the lines in
his employer's ears! Greatly astonished was that gentleman, for previous to this outburst Mr. Timrod's manner
towards him had been marked by a studied reserve; nor
was it the poet's habit to declaim his rhymes, even among
his intimates.

SONS OF THE UNION!

I.

> " Sons of the Union, rise !
> Stand ye not recreant by, and see
> The brightest star in Freedom's galaxy
>   Flung sullied from the skies !

II.

" Hosts of the martyred brave !
Bend ye not your pure spirits from the clouds,
Indignant at the darkness that enshrouds
  The land ye died to save ?

III.

" Sons of the brave ! shall ye,
Basely submissive, crouch to faction's slaves ?
No ! rather lay ye down in glorious graves :
  'Tis easy to die free !

IV.

" And who the foes that dare
Flout the brave banner of a mighty land,
Which floating in a thousand fields, hath fanned
  The brow of victory there ?

V.

" Laid they the scheme of blood,
Blasting the hope of ages yet to come,
Beneath some Temple's consecrated dome,
  With tears and prayers to God ?

VI.

" No ! In the wassail hall,
Draining the maddening wine-cup, while the cries
Of brutal drunkenness affront the skies,
  They planned their country's fall !

VII.

" God ! do thy high decrees
Doom that our fathers' blood was shed in vain,
And that our glorious Union's sacred chain
  Be snapped by foes like these ?

VIII.

" Sons of the Union, rise !
Stand ye not recreant by, and see
The highest star in Freedom's galaxy
Flung sullied from the skies ! "

The intense bitterness of tone displayed in this lyric, will be understood and partially excused by those who reflect that it was, in truth, *a campaign production*, written during the heat and in the midst of the recriminations of the most savage political contest this country had known previous to the year 1860.

But William Timrod was not a mere writer of miscellaneous verses. I learn from the best authority that he composed a Drama in Five Acts, which he regarded, as *par excellence*, the literary labor of his life! By some strange fatality the manuscript of this play was lost—a misfortune which his son continually and bitterly lamented.

His patriotism and popularity with the chiefs of his own party procured, after a time, for William Timrod an honorable position in the Charleston Custom House. How long he retained this office I have had no means of ascertaining.

In 1835 he was elected to the command of the *German Fusileers*, an ancient and distinguished volunteer corps of Charleston, composed of Germans and men of German descent, and marched with them to garrison the town of St. Augustine, in Florida, against the attacks of the Seminole Indians. Exposure, hardship, and protracted labor, brought on a disease of which, about two years after his return to Charleston, he died.

Thus perished in his prime a man of remarkable mental vigor and versatility. What he might have done under fairer auspices, it would be useless to inquire. His name henceforth must live chiefly in the reputation of his son, his "blue-eyed Harry," of whom he wrote so feelingly, and with such prescient insight.

The latter obtained his primary education at one of the best schools in Charleston. There I first made his acquaintance—an acquaintance which similarity of tastes, and an equality of age, soon ripened into friendship. My seat in the school-room being next to his, I well remember the exultation with which he showed me, one morning, his earliest consecutive attempt at verse-making.

It was a ballad of stirring adventures, and sanguinary catastrophe! But I thought it perfect—wonderful—and so, naturally, did he. Our "down East" schoolmaster, however, (all whose duties except those connected with penal inflictions, were left to his ushers, for our Principal united the morals of Pecksniff with the learning of Squeers), could boast of no turn for sentiment, and having remarked us hobnobbing, meanly assaulted us in the rear, effectually quenching for the time all æsthetic enthusiasm.

An early teacher of Timrod, who really knew and appreciated his character and mind, describes him when a boy, as "modest and diffident, with a nervous utterance, but with melody ever in his heart and on his lips. Though always slow of speech, he was yet, like Burns, quick to learn. The chariot wheels might jar in the gate through which he tried to drive his winged steeds, but the horses were of celestial temper, and the car of purest gold." Shy, but neither melancholy nor morose, he was passionate, impulsive, eagerly ambitious, with a thirst for knowledge hard to satiate. But too close a devotion to books did not destroy the natural lightness and simplicity of youth. He mingled freely with his comrades, all of whom respected, while some dearly loved him. At that time of life he was physically active and

vigorous, and delighted in every sort of rough out-door
sport; in leaping, running, wrestling, swimming, and even
in *fighting.* More than once I have known him to engage in
a desperate *affaire d'honneur*, the issue of which was decided
by a primitive species of science that would have disgusted
the orthodox "ring."

"How unspeakably," exclaims one of his associates,
"Timrod rejoiced in the weekly holiday, with its long ram-
bles through field and wood! And this taste strengthened
with his growth. 'The sweet security of streets,' that Elia
loved, had no charm for him.

"Born in a city, pent up in its dusty avenues, he longed
for the untrammeled freedom of the country. He doted upon
its waving fields, its deep blue skies, and the glory of the
changing seasons. These formed his special delight, because in them he instinctively recognized his best teachers.
Face to face with Nature he had no fears, no misgivings;
always a beneficent mother, she 'nursed him with the milk
of a better time,' and through all his years he leaned on her
breast with the loving trustfulness of a little child."

When about sixteen or seventeen, Timrod was prepared to
enter college. By the advice, and under the influence of
friends, he matriculated at the University of Georgia. There,
his vivid intelligence and scholarly ardor soon began to display themselves.

He sought to enlarge his culture and refine his taste by
habitual commerce with the classics. By the horror and
gloom of the Æschylean drama he appears to have been
revolted; but "sad Electra's poet" charmed him; he revelled
in the elegant art of Virgil; and of the graces of Horace and
Catullus he never wearied.

From the fountain of English letters he quaffed unceas-
ingly. Nevertheless, his reading was more exact than varied.

His unerring critical tact rejected the false and meretricious; but for authors of his deliberate choice, his affection daily increased.

There, too, at the University, his poetical gifts commenced to "burgeon" luxuriantly. "A large part," said he, laughing, "of my leisure at college, was occupied in the composition of love verses, frantic or tender. Every pretty girl's face I met acted upon me like an inspiration! I fancied myself a sublimated Turk (when these faces were reproduced in day-dreams) though walking an ideal, and therefore innocent, Harem of young Beauties." Some of the cleverest of these love-songs were published in "*The Charleston Evening News,*" over a fictitious signature. They became, *locally*, quite popular, and in one instance, to the author's intense delight, his verses were set to music.

Unluckily, the young poet's college career was brought to a sudden close, in part by temporary ill health, and yet more perhaps, by the "*res angusta domi.*" Forced thus to leave his *alma mater*, his brow unadorned by academic honors—he left her, at all events, possessed of valuable stores of learning, and with an intellect unusually well drilled, and disciplined.

And now the battle of existence opened in grim earnest; for him an unending struggle with evil fates; a conflict in which, overcome again and again, thrown to earth as fast as he struggled up therefrom, he found but few kindly hands to help him; and yet came off more than conqueror, through untold resources of his liberal nature.

Timrod's first move upon returning to his native city, was to enter, as a student, the office of that distinguished lawyer, James L. Petigru, Esq. Often in those days, he frequented the rooms of the "Charleston Mechanic's Library Association," where at irregular intervals an informal debating club of young men was in the habit of assembling.

Timrod was fond of argument, but as an extemporaneous speaker, he had not, as already hinted, inherited his father's facility of language and illustration.   Unless excited upon some theme of special moment, he hesitated, stammered, and was continually at a loss for words to embody his ideas; although the ideas themselves were never commonplace or trivial.

On the other hand, he was an admirable reader, even if his style *did* sometimes verge upon the theatrical.

I can see him now as he appeared in his early manhood, repeating in a deep, musical bass voice, his favorite "ode" on "Intimations of Immortality from Recollections of early Childhood."   Short of stature, but broad-chested, and compactly formed, with his superb head well set upon shoulders, erect, and thrown back in haughty grace—his gray eyes flashing, and his swarthy face one glow of intense emotion— it was impossible to listen to him without catching some spark of his fiery enthusiasm.

In 1848–9, having assumed the *nom de plume* of "AGLÄUS,"* he commenced a series of contributions to the " *The Southern Literary Messenger,*" then edited by that kindly and accomplished scholar, John R. Thompson, Esq.   His genius was gradually maturing, and his art-culture with it!

Let any one who can, examine the back numbers of " *The Messenger,*" from 1849 to the year 1853, containing as they do, the best of our author's earlier poems, and I think it will be acknowledged, that despite some superficial marks of imitation, the verses display both individuality and power. One piece especially, entitled " *The Past,*" was so full of a subdued thoughtfulness and beauty, that after having been republished by scores of periodicals, it came under the notice

---

* The name of a minor pastoral poet of Greece.

of a distinguished Northern gentleman, himself an author, who, corresponding with a friend in Charleston, expressed his hearty admiration of the lines, making inquiry at the same time in reference to the poet, and his circumstances. The letter was shown to Timrod, and its encouraging effect was greater and more permanent, than could be understood by any person not gifted in some degree with the suscepti- bility of genius.

Every poet, in the morning of his career among the masters of song that have preceded him, is apt to select some special object of his imaginative and artistic worship. In those days, Timrod looked up to Wordsworth as his poetical guide and exemplar. With a constant and loving earnestness, he studied his works, caught their spirit of simplicity and truth, and thus laid the foundation of a style, which, however modified by after-studies and experience, was remarkable to the last for its pure Saxon vigor, its terseness, lucidity, and unpretending grace.

Finding the law distasteful,* Timrod threw aside his

---

* Alluding to this period, *Judge Bryan* says (in a private com- munication), " Timrod was too wholly a poet to keep company long with so relentless, rugged, and exacting a mistress as the law! As a curious illustration of the abstraction and reverie which so often absorbed the poet, he told me that Mr. Petigru sent him on *one* occasion to take a message to a certain Factor on the Bay. But as ill-luck would have it, when he had gone half way he found he had forgotten, if indeed he ever really knew, the message entrusted to his care. What was to be done? He could only return, and, with as bold a face as possible, acknow- ledged his misfortune.

" On his doing so, Mr. Petigru saluted him, very much excited, in his highest squeaking voice, ' *Why Harry, you are a fool!* ' And, added our poet friend to me, ' I would have been a fool to

Chitty and Blackstone, and determined to renew his classical studies, so as to make himself competent as a College Professor or a Tutor in families. *This* he conscientiously did, and in due time, no Professorship opening to him, he accepted the post of teacher of children in the household of a Carolina planter, with whom he remained for several consecutive seasons.

Henceforth, for a decade at least, the labors of a tutor were the sole means upon which he relied for subsistence. He went from household to household, faithfully instructing the youths placed under him; longing often, no doubt, and passionately longing, for a different field of toil or action; yet not ungrateful for the leisure hours allowed him, in which he could cultivate his own mind, and exercise his imagination in writing.

In this narrow round of simple duties and pleasures, his youth was spent. At times there came to him from the outer world sounds which stirred his deeper heart, and quickened his pulse into momentary unison with that feverish life that he felt was burning beyond him. But he repressed the desire which even the most languid must feel at intervals, to be of the world, doers as well as thinkers, and travelled along life's common way, conscious only of his own pure aims; and, perhaps, somewhat dimly conscious as yet of his extraordinary powers.

Whenever in spring or winter the holiday season came round, Timrod, forgetting his cares, would joyfully rush down to Charleston to be welcomed by a small *coterie* of friends with demonstrative cordiality.

Among these was William Gilmore Simms, who delighted

Mr. Petigru to the end of my days, even had I revealed in after-life the genius of a Milton or a Shakspeare!'"

to gather round him the younger literary men of his acquaintance, and to discuss with them the thousand and one topics
connected with art and letters. Many and jovial were the
"little suppers " of which we partook at his pleasant town
residence, none of the guests, perhaps, enjoying themselves
as vividly as Timrod, whose excitable temperament, and
keenly social proclivities, made his whole heart expand in
the companionship of those he loved and trusted.

It was at one of these *petits soupers* that the idea originated
of starting a Monthly Magazine in Charleston, which might
serve as an exponent of Southern talent and culture. The
idea speedily assumed a definite form. An enterprising,
intelligent, and popular bookseller then doing business in
the city, Mr. John Russell, was induced to take the practical
management of the work, which, in honor of its founder,
was called "*Russell's Magazine.*" The editorship devolved
upon the present writer, supported by a small corps of clever,
but by no means very regular *collaborateurs*.

On the first day of April (ominous coincidence!), the initial
number of "*Russell's*" appeared. It was neatly printed in the
style of "*Blackwood*," and the general impression, typo-
graphical and intellectual, made by it, was certainly favorable. In the long run, however, a want of capital proved in
this case, as it must prove in all similar cases, fatal !
"Eleemosynary literature," as Mr. Simms used to call it,
can never be permanently maintained; nor, were that possible, would it in all likelihood be *worth* maintaining. Nevertheless, we struggled on with the work for years; nor until
the completion of the *fourth* volume, did we confess ourselves beaten, and retire with our defunct "Maga" from the
public view. The lost means and labor expended on this
Monthly I have always looked upon as counterbalanced by
the facilities for publication it afforded to our gifted local

authors; especially to Timrod, some of whose most charming and characteristic poems were composed for its pages.

Such, for instance, was "*The Arctic Voyager*," in which we detect for the first time in our author's art, the influence of Tennyson, not superseding, but harmoniously blending with the earlier influence of Wordsworth. Such also, were his "*Præceptor Amat*," and "*The Rhapsody of a Southern Winter's Night*." Among the briefer lyrics carelessly thrown off by him at this period, we find in "*Russell's*" the fragment of a song faithfully reflecting one of those sombre moods, which, owing to circumstances rather than temperament, were, alas! too frequent with him. It is in a loose, reckless measure, rhythmically unlike any other production of the writer, and since this volume does not include it, we will quote the lines. They have a psychological, if not poetical, significance:

> " Is it gone forever, my gay spring time ?
>   Shall I never be as I was then—
> And this dead heart which once beat so wildly,
>   Who shall wake it—*can* it wake again ?

> " From the sea where joy lies buried, shall not
>   Something like its shadow flutter up ?
> The bright wine of life, I quaffed so madly,
>   Hath it left no sweetness in the cup ?

> " Yet it is not that my youth has perished—
>   If I count by years I am not old ;
> Of that youth I stripped the buds too early,
>   And its leafless stem is all I hold.

> " Oh ! doth no new Autumn yet await me ?
>   Thus I question *Fate*, but *Fate* is mute.
> *Is* it Autumn ? where is Autumn's foliage,
>   And its golden store of luscious fruit ? "

In the same periodical we find a few specimens of Timrod's powers as a *prose* essayist and critic. Discussing that venerable question, "What is Poetry?" he shows a strong, clear judgment, and a thorough appreciation of his subject in all its phases.

"As we recall," he says, "the various attempts to describe, in a single definition, those operations of the human mind upon itself and the world without, which, *incarnated* in language, we term *poetry*, we are reminded of a childish search, actually commenced by ourselves, after *the pot of gold which is said to be buried at the foot of the rainbows.*"

Elsewhere he remarks:

"Poetry does not deal in pure abstractions. However abstract be his thought, the poet is compelled, by his passion-fused imagination, to give it life, form, or color.

"Hence the necessity of employing the *sensuous or concrete* words of the language, and hence the exclusion of long words, which in English are nearly all purely and austerely *abstract*, from the poetic vocabulary. Whenever a poet drags a number of these words into his verse, we say that he is prosaic ; meaning by this, *not* that he has written prose, nor that he is simply deficient in spirit and vivacity; but that he has not used the *legitimate* language of poetry; he has written something which is only distinguished from the ordinary dead-level of unimpassioned prose by the feet upon which it crawls."

And again: "The ground of the poetic character is a more than ordinary sensibility. From this characteristic of the poet results what we regard as an essential characteristic of poetry, namely, the medium of strong emotion through which poetry looks at its objects, and in which, to borrow a chemical metaphor of Arthur Hallam, 'it holds them all fused.' Hence, again, is derived a third peculiarity in the *language* of poetry, which, with a difference in the *degree*, not the *kind,* of its force—arising from an imagination more than usually vivid—is the language natural to men in a state of excitement, is sensuous, picturesque, and impassioned!"

From these extracts, and the extracts about to follow, an imperfect glimpse may be obtained of the writer's poetic creed.

Timrod, as was natural with a disciple of Wordsworth, enthusiastically admired the Sonnet. He defends it against the assaults of a large body of depreciators with admirable skill and effect.

"The Sonnet," he begins, "has been called artificial. It *is* artificial, but only as *all* forms of verse are artificial. There are persons who imagine poetry to be the result of a sort of mystical inspiration, scarcely to be subjected to the bounds of time or space! Others, regarding it as the outgushing of a present emotion, cannot conceive how the poet, carried on by the 'divine afflatus,' should always contrive to rein in his Pegasus at a certain goal. All this is ridiculous!

"If the poet have his hour of inspiration (though we are so sick of the *cant* of which this word has been the fruitful source, that we dislike to use it), it is *not* during the act of composition.

"A distinction must be made between the moment when the great thought first breaks upon the mind,

> ' Leaving in the brain
> A rocking and a ringing,'

and the hour of patient, elaborate execution. It is in the *conception* only that the poet is the *vates!* In the labor of putting that conception into words, he is simply the *artist.*

"A great poet has defined poetry to be 'emotion recollected in tranquillity.' No man with grief in his heart could sit straightway down to strain that grief through iambics! No man exulting in a delirium of joy, ever bubbles into anapæsts! Were this so, the poet would be the most wonderful of improvisators; and perhaps poetry would be no better than what improvisations usually are.

" There can be no doubt that much of the most passionate verse in the English, or any other language, has been

> ' *Thoughtfully* fitted to the Orphean lyre.

" The act of composition is indeed attended with an emotion peculiar to itself and to the poet: and this emotion is sufficient of itself to give a glow and richness to the poet's language; yet it leaves him, at the same time, in such command of his faculties, that he is able to choose his words almost as freely, though by no means as *deliberately*, as the painter chooses his colors.

" We are inclined to think that the emotion of the poet somewhat resembles in its metaphysical character those inexplicable feelings with which we all witness a tragic performance on the stage—feelings which, even while they rend the heart, are always attended by a large amount of vivid pleasure.

"It would be easy to multiply quotations in confirmation of our remarks. Wordsworth speaks of himself as

> ' Not used to make
> A present joy the matter of his song ;'

and Matthew Arnold separates, as we have separated, 'the hour of insight' from the hour of labor.

' We cannot kindle when we will
　　That fire which in the heart resides ;
The spirit bloweth, and is still ;
　　In mystery our soul abides :
But tasks in hours of insight willed,
　　May be through hours of gloom fulfilled.'

" Is it not also a significant fact that the best love-verses
have been written by men who, at the time of writing them,
had long passed that age during which love is warmest, and
the heart most susceptible ?

　　　*　　　*　　　*　　　*　　　*　　　*　　　*

" The very restriction so much complained of in the
Sonnet, the artist knows to be an advantage. It forces him
to condensation, and if it sometimes induces a poetaster to
stretch a thought to the finest tenuity, what argument is that
against the Sonnet ? As well might Jones object to the
violin of Paganini, because Smith, his neighbor, is a wretched
fiddler !

" The Sonnet is designed, as it is peculiarly fitted, for the
development of a single thought, emotion, or picture.

" It is governed by another law not less imperative than
that which determines its length. We know not how else
to characterize it but as the law of *unity !* In a poem made
up of a series of stanzas, the thought in the first stanza sug-
gests the thought in the second, and both may be equally
important. The concluding stanza may have wandered as
far in its allusions from the opening stanza, as the last from
the first sentence in an essay. In other words, the poet has
the liberty of rambling somewhat, if his fancy so dispose
him.

" Now, in the Sonnet this suggestive progress from one

thought to another is inadmissible. It *must* consist of one leading idea around which the others are grouped for purposes of illustration only.

*   *   *   *   *   *   *

"We claim for the Sonnet, as represented in English literature, a proud distinction. We could gather from it a greater body of tersely expressed and valuable thought, than from any equal quantity of those fugitive verses, the laws of which are less exacting.

"It abounds in those 'great thoughts, grave thoughts,' which, embodied in lines of wonderful pregnancy, haunt the memory forever.

"Brief as the Sonnet is, the whole power of a poet has sometimes been exemplified within its narrow bounds as completely as within the compass of an epic! Thought is independent of space; and it would hardly be an exaggeration to say that the poet—the minister of thought—enjoys an equal independence.

"*To-day, his stature reaches the sky; to-morrow, he will shut himself up in the bell of a tulip or the cup of a lily!*"

In 1860, a small volume, comprising the best of Timrod's verses, produced during the eight or nine years previous, was issued by *Ticknor & Fields*, of Boston. A better *first* volume of the kind has seldom appeared anywhere. It was welcomed outside the author's immediate circle by a few cultivated Southern editors, and some even of the critics of the North did not hesitate to commend it.

For example, "*The Tribune*" said: "These poems are worthy of a wide audience. They form a welcome offering to the common literature of our country. The author, whose name promises to be better known from this specimen of his powers, betrays a genuine poetic instinct in the selection of his themes, and has treated them with a lively, delicate fancy, and a graceful beauty of expression." *

The most elaborate performance in this book, indeed the longest poem Timrod ever wrote, is called " *A Vision of Poesy.*" Its purpose is to show, in the subtle development of a highly gifted imaginative nature, the true laws which underlie and determine the noblest uses of the poetical faculty. The subject is one of difficulty, demanding for its successful treatment not only an originally comprehensive and subtle mind, but no little knowledge of psychological truths, and the philosophy of intellectual growth.

Imagination, descriptive capacity, and metaphysical insight are active in elucidating the theme; and the result is a *generally* pleasing and impressive work, marred, however, by a too evident lack of harmony and unity of parts, proceed-

---

* Such comparatively slender recognition as *this,* of course fell short of the poet's anticipations of success.

Apropos of this volume, a kindly but discerning critic observes : —" The book was full of promise; it gave evidence of considerable culture, of a lively fancy, a delicate, and at times vigorous imagination, and a rare artistic power. Yet it fell *almost* dead from the press !

" The few who had real critical taste, a genuine and native appreciation of excellence, felt and expressed their admiration ; but the public had no niche for him, not, at least, until he had achieved success, and success was to him a bitter need, for not his *living* merely, but his *life* was staked upon it !

" And the disappointment was peculiarly keen, because just at this juncture his other resources had failed. He had surrendered everything to his art.

" He had hoped, earnestly and justly, to make a little rift through which the light of popular favor might steal, and now only clouds and shadows were closing round him."—*From a Lecture on Timrod, and his Poetry, by Dr. J. Dickson Bruns.*

ing from the fact that the narrative was composed in sections, and after the lapse of periods so long between the different *bouts* of composition, that much of the original fervor of both conception and execution must have evaporated.*

The metrical form of *"The Vision"* is well chosen, and admirably managed. It is that employed by Shakspeare in his *"Venus and Adonis,"* by Spenser in his *"Astrophel,"* and Cowley in his least ambiguous verses; being, briefly, the elegiac metre, with its alternate rhyme, so warmly defended by Dryden, ending in the terseness of the rhyming couplet, in which the picture should be closed, or the sense clinched.

But. of course, the chief merit of *"The Vision"* is to be found in the unfolding of its leading idea. To accomplish this, Timrod has introduced a story of the mental progress of a youth, possessed of brilliant poetic gifts, which are partially nullified, in the end, by the joint operation of mistaken views of his art, and a morbid subjectivity of nature, fatal to the acknowledgment of his genius by humanity at large.

The story is divided into *three Parts ;* each devoted to some particular phase of its hero's experience.

As the boy's "mystical thought," his desire to comprehend something of the secrets of the Universe, suddenly bursts into utterance, he turns to his mother, she who had taught him that "most beautiful of all things"—speech, —saying:

---

* After all, *"The Vision of Poesy"* cannot be considered as in any sense a mature effort.

Excepting a few passages which declare themselves to the intelligent reader, the poem was written at a comparatively early age.

" But, mother! while our human words are rife
   To us with meaning, other sounds there be,
   Which seem and *are* the language of a life
   Around, yet unlike ours—winds talk, the sea
   Murmurs articulately, and the sky
   Listens and answers, tho' inaudibly.

" By stream and spring, in glades and woodlands lone,
   Beside our very cot I've gathered flowers
   Inscribed with signs and characters unknown ;
   But the frail scrolls still baffle all my powers :
   What is this language, and where is the key
   That opes its weird and wondrous mystery ? "

The poor mother, from whom sordid cares and a life-time
of the trouble which attaches to material toil had removed
her own childhood and its visions, very far away, is first
puzzled, and then alarmed, by these strange questionings.
She recalls a marvel that attended her child's birth, once
considered an omen of good, but now converted by super-
stitious fancy into a curse and prophecy of disaster! Trem-
ulously she tells her son this story of his birth-night.

Thenceforth the boy keeps his strange imaginings, which
he perceives cannot be understood, locked in the depths of
his own consciousness.

Meanwhile, the quiet days speed on, and in due course of
time "the thoughtful boy blossoms into youth." The
"dream" which had haunted his childhood becomes the
"deathless need" of his maturer years. A spirit of unrest,
yet of beauty, it drives him to seek the heart of lonely
forests, and to wander over distant hills.

He communes, not only with the waters, the sky, and the
flowers, but becomes the familiar of those wild creatures to
whom the sight of ordinary men brings terror and dismay :

> " The eagle knew him as she knew the blast,
> And the deer did not flee him as he passed."

There is a particular nook in the forest, to which the youth continually repairs. One night he comes to his favorite spot. The trees, "high and hushed," rise solemnly about him, and

> " Silent, but not as slumbering, all things there
> Wore to the youth's aroused imagination
> An air of deep and solemn expectation."

The presentiment is not a vain instinct merely, for there the *Spirit of Poesy* reveals herself to him, and in burning words she speaks of the glory, dignity, and loveliness of her divine art and mission.

This is, I think, the most thoughtful and highly-wrought portion of the poem.

Part the Second forms the connecting link between the opening and the concluding events of the poet's career.

It is written in blank verse, and with characteristic care and skill. Here is a specimen of its felicity of style:

> " The story came to me—it recks not whence—
> In fragments. Oh! if I could tell it all—
> If human speech indeed could tell it all—
> 'Twere not a whit less wondrous, than if I
> Should find, untouched in leaf and stem, and bright
> As when it bloomed three thousand years ago
> On some Idalian slope, a perfect rose.
> Alas! a leaf or two, and they perchance
> Scarce worth the hiving—one or two dead leaves
> Are the sole harvest of a summer's toil."

*   *   *   *   *   *   *

" *I have heard*
Somewhere of some dead monarch, from the tomb,
Where he had slept a century and more,
Brought forth, that when the coffin was laid bare,
Albeit the body in its mouldering robes
Was fleshless, yet one feature still remained
Perfect, or perfect seemed at least ; the eyes
Gleamed for a second on the startled crowd,
And then went out in ashes ! *   Even thus,
The story, when I drew it from the grave,
Where it had lain so long, did seem, I thought,
Not wholly lifeless ; but even while I gazed,
To fix its features on my heart, and called
The world to wonder with me, lo ! it proved
I looked upon a corpse ! "

As for the poet himself, he goes into "the busy world to
seek his fate." In many lands, and to many peoples he
sings

' Of all he thought, and all he dreamed and hoped
   But—or because the people were intent

---

* Tennyson, in his *"Aylmer's Field,"* a tale which appeared
after the publication of " *The Vision,"* makes use of this very
image, as follows :

" Dust are our frames ; and gilded dust, our pride
   Looks only for a moment whole and sound ;
   Like that long-buried body of the king
   Found lying with his arms and ornaments,
   Which at a touch of light, an air of heaven,
   Slipt into ashes and was found no more."

Of these two verses, assuredly that of the younger and obscurer
poet is the more striking.

On other themes, or they were not prepared
To dream his dreams, or think the thoughts *he* thought,
Or—that not being as other men, he touched
No chord that vibrated from heart to heart,
The peoples would not hear, or hearing, turned
And went their way unheedful!"

Thus the inevitable climax approaches, failure, disappointment, death. A love "not wisely placed," a genius not
wisely directed, these induce a "sickness of the soul," and,
gray before his time, his ideals shattered, and his true passion unappreciated, if not scorned, the poet seeks his ancient
home, in order that he may look on its beloved scenes again
before he himself is called hence, to be beheld of men no
more.

There is something in this description of the bard's latter
and darker days; of his mournful disenchantment, his mild,
yet profound despair, which is singularly pathetic; the
more pathetic indeed, as the catastrophe, losing for an instant its idealism, becomes, as it were, half subjective in its
nature, and points to the author's own melancholy doom!

With the instinct of right art and genuine feeling, Timrod
has taken care not to make his hero a bitter misanthrope,
nor to leave him skeptical of the joy and glory "which *may*
hereafter be revealed."

Even his poetic work and mission are portrayed as not
utterly barren and fruitless.

Exalted is the moral, beautiful the philosophy embodied
in these concluding lines:

" Thy life hath not been wholly without use,
   Albeit that use is partly hidden now.
   In thy unmingled scorn of any truce
   With this world's specious falsehoods, often thou

Hast uttered through some all unworldly song,
Truths that for man might else have slumbered long.

" And these not always vainly on the crowd
Have fallen ; some are cherished now, and some,
In mystic phrases wrapped as in a shroud,
Wait the diviner, *who as yet is dumb*
Upon the breast of God—the gate of birth
Closed on a dreamless ignorance of earth.

" And therefore, though thy name shall pass away,
Even as a cloud that hath wept all its showers,
Yet as that cloud shall live again one day
In the glad grass and in the happy flowers ;
So in thy thoughts, though clothed in sweeter rhymes,
Thy life shall bear its flowers in future times ! "

Of the minor poems which followed " *The Vision,*" it is
unnecessary to speak in detail. The ablest of them have been
included in the present edition.

We now come to the period of the War, during the first
months of which Timrod remained chiefly in Charleston, serv-
ing his country a thousand times more effectually with his
pen, than he could possibly have served her with his *sword.*

It was in 1861 that he inaugurated that remarkable *series*
of poems, suggested by the incidents of the great conflict,
tragic or triumphant, in which he struck a higher and
firmer note than any hitherto elicited from his lyre.

" *Ethnogenesis* " is the worthy leader of these sustained and
earnest strains. The dignity and calmness of its tone, cov-
ering unsounded depths of ardor and enthusiasm ; its subtle
grace of imagination, feeling, and imagery, and the *crisp*
purity of the versification are so artistically blended in this
ODE, that one cannot criticise, but must simply and hon-

estly admire it! The concluding stanza cannot now be read, at least by any Southerner, without a yearning and passion- ate regret. How the Poet's cordial sympathetic temper re- veals itself in these lines, which came more naturally to him than visions of violence and blood!

> " But let our fears—if fears we have—be still,
>   And turn us to the future! Could we climb
> Some mighty Alp, and view the coming time,
>   The rapturous sight would fill
>   Our eyes with happy tears!
>   Not only for the glories which the years
> Shall bring us ; not for lands from sea to sea,
> And wealth, and power, and peace, though these shall be ;
> *But for the distant peoples we shall bless,*
> *And the hushed murmurs of a world's distress ;*
>   For, to give labor to the poor,
>   This whole sad planet o'er,
> And save from want and crime the humblest door,
>   Is one among the many ends for which
>   God makes us great and rich !
>   The hour perchance is not yet wholly ripe
>   When all shall own it, but the type
> Whereby we shall be known in every land,
> Is that vast Gulf which laves our Southern strand,
> And through the cold, untempered Ocean pours
> Its genial streams, that far-off Arctic shores
> *May sometimes catch upon the softened breeze*
> *Strange Tropic warmth, and* HINTS *of summer seas !* "

That resonant lyric, "*A Call to Arms,*" succeeded "*Ethno-genesis.*" It contains one of the few palpable conceits I can recall, which would seem not merely admissible, but charm- ing.

And next appeared a Tyrtaean strain indeed, I mean the

lines on " *Carolina ;* " —lines destined perhaps to outlive the political vitality of the State, whose antique fame they celebrate.

I read them first, and was thrilled by their power and pathos, upon a stormy March evening in Fort Sumter! Walking along the battlements, under the red light of a tempestuous sunset, the wind steadily and loudly blowing from off the bar across the tossing and moaning waste of waters, driven inland; with scores of gulls and white sea-birds flying and shrieking round me,—those wild voices of Nature mingled strangely with the rhythmic roll and beat of the poet's impassioned music. The very spirit, or dark genius, of the troubled scene, appeared to take up, and to repeat such verses as—

> " I hear a murmur as of waves
>   That grope their way through sunless caves,
>   Like bodies struggling in their graves,
>   Carolina!
>
> " And now it deepens ; slow and grand
>   It swells, as rolling to the land,
>   An ocean broke upon the strand,
>   Carolina!
>
> " Shout ! let it reach the startled Huns!
>   And roar with all thy festal guns!
>   It is the answer of thy sons!
>   Carolina ! "

At last, influenced by these and other poems of kindred force and fire, the public awoke to a sense of Timrod's unusual merit. Towards the close of 1862, a project was formed in Charleston, with the view of having an illustrated and highly embellished edition of Timrod's works published in

the city of London. Vizetelli, an Englishman of Italian
blood, and an artist of some eminence, then the Southern
War Correspondent of " *The London News*," offered to supply original illustrations of his own ; and so warm was the
support the proposition met with from some of the chief
men and most opulent merchants of the State, that but little
doubt was entertained of its immediate and practical realiza-
tion.*

The poet, now in jubilant spirits, collected all the compositions of which his taste approved, and had them printed
near him, so that correct proof-sheets might be sent to the
publishers across the Ocean. Among his war-lyrics he placed
some poems, also lately written, of a more subjective tone and
character, for example—" *Katie*," and " *An Exotic ;* " both
of which, from their references to English history, scenery,
and manners, were likely to be appreciated in the "mother-
land." The former ("*Katie*") is dedicated to the lady
whom Timrod subsequently married ; and is full of charming details of her girlish walks through the streets of old
Bury St. Edmunds; and of her innocent holiday pastime in
the lovely country around it. The piece is almost pre-
Raphaelite in the delicious minuteness of its word-painting.

But alas! that evil Fortune, that haunted our poet from
the cradle to the grave, that never left him for a season, but
to return darker, grimmer, more ruthless than before ; decreed that the publication scheme, which had aroused his
best hopes and energies, by promising to make his genius
known in the great centre of·English literary art, should
prove but a mockery and delusion after all!

---

* The intention, we learn, was " to present this edition to the
author ; the object being to bring him, in the highest style, before
the world, and at the same time to secure to him a modest compe-
tence."

In the hurry and pressure of great events, the solitary singer, "pipe he never so sweetly and boldly," was quite forgotten.

Those gentlemen who had played the kindly *rôle* of patrons, found their own weightier interests, and no doubt the interests of the Commonwealth, endangered; therefore what more natural than the consignment by them of the poet's expectations to that region of "Limbo," which is said to engulf so many "vows unredeemed, and visions unfulfilled?"

Although no reason was ever given to Timrod, for the abandonment of this scheme, he could form his own conjectures on the subject. Every hour his once bright anticipations grew duller, until ultimately they smouldered out, one by one, in the anguish, solitude, and bitterness of his soul.*

---

* *Years afterwards* Timrod, on *two* occasions, alludes (in his correspondence) to the manner in which the scheme had died out.

"The great plan," he writes, "for publishing an illustrated edition of my poems has (*I believe*) evaporated in smoke! So fades, so languishes, grows dim and dies, the hope of every poet who has not money!"

In another, and more recent letter, he thus refers to the subject: "The project of publishing my poems in England *has been silently but altogether dropped!* An unspeakable disappointment! but I try to bear my lot—the lot," he adds, with a momentary bitterness, "of all impecunious poets."

Next to the poet himself, this disappointment in regard to the English edition of his works, fell most heavily upon *his mother*. Perhaps in HER case, the disappointment was even greater, since in extreme old age, she could scarcely look forward to the sharing of any possible literary triumph of her son in the future.

The mention of her here, gives us the opportunity of quoting some passages from an interesting letter descriptive of this lady's

It was soon after the bloody and desperate battle of Shiloh, that Timrod joined the army of the West, as "War Correspondent" of the Charleston "*Mercury.*"

---

family, her character, intellect, etc., written by one who knew her in all the most sacred and intimate relations of existence.

Such as read them may think that our former assertion, or rather, inference, that the poet's genius was wholly derived from his *father*, ought to be considerably qualified.

"Henry Timrod's mother was the daughter of Mr. Charles Prince, a citizen of Charleston, S. C., and one of whom, at his death, my father said, 'he was the most upright and honest man I ever knew.'

"Mr. Prince was the son of English parents, who emigrated to Carolina just before the breaking out of the Revolution.

"He married a Miss French, whose father, of the Swiss family of French, came over from Switzerland, and fought as an officer of Republican artillery, during the whole war."

    *   *   *   *   *   *   *   *   *

"My father (Wm. H. Timrod), at the early age of *nineteen*, married Miss Prince, then a young and beautiful girl of sixteen or seventeen. The perfection of her face and form caught the poet's *fancy ;* the perfection of her character won and kept his HEART through the twenty-six years of their married life.

"It was from *her*, more than from his gifted father, that my brother (Henry Timrod) derived that intense, passionate love of Nature which so distinguished him. Its sights and sounds always afforded her extreme delight. Shall I ever forget the almost childish rapture she testified, when, after a residence in the pent-up city all her life, she removed with me to the country ? A walk in the woods to her was food and drink, and the sight of a green field was joy inexpressible.

"From my earliest childhood, I can remember her love for flowers and trees and for the stars ; how she would call our attention to the glintings of the sunshine through the leaves; to the afternoon's lights and shadows, as they slept quietly, side by side; and even to a streak of moonlight on the floor.

"The story," says Dr. Bruns, in his masterly Lecture on the Poet and his genius, "the story of his camp life would furnish a theme for mirth, if our laughter were not choked by tears! One can scarcely conceive a situation more hopelessly wretched than that of this child, as it were, suddenly flung down into the heart of that stormy retreat, and tossed like a straw on the crest of those crimson waves, from which he escaped as by a miracle."

Out of the refluent tides of blood, from under the smoke of conflict, and the sickening fumes of slaughter, he staggered homeward, half blinded, bewildered, with a dull red mist before his eyes, and a shuddering horror at heart.

But now, as if some beneficent spirit, who had long witnessed his troubles, and also the calm, brave front of patience wherewith he opposed them, had resolved that at the last, some sweetness should be mingled with the wormwood of his life, he exchanged the turmoil of his recent deadly experience, for what to him must have seemed, by comparison, a very Eden of peace and happiness !

Removing to Columbia, S. C., whither his family had preceded him, he was enabled to become (but through what precise means I cannot tell) part proprietor and associate editor of the "*South Carolinian,*" a daily paper, published

---

"She would sit absorbed, watching the tree-branches as they waved in the wind, and say, 'Don't they seem to be whispering to each other in a language of their own ?'

"To this strong love of Nature, she added so correct a judgment in all things ; so much sound practical sense ; such self-abnegation and entire devotion to those she loved ; and such sweetness, forbearance, gentleness, that I think I can truly say, she was one of the most perfect characters I ever knew !

"Her children loved her with a devotion rarely given even to parents."

in the Capital, which promised to yield him a moderate, and what was better still, a permanent support.

Thus provided for, as he fondly believed, Timrod saw the possibility of realizing what had long been the dearest wish of his soul. Miss Kate Goodwin, the "Katie" of his poetic visions, she whose charms are embalmed in his delicate yet glowing verse, came to this country from England in the spring of 1860. She accompanied her father, who came to visit his son (Mr. George M. Goodwin, long settled as a merchant in Charleston, S. C., and married to one of Henry Timrod's sisters), and also, in accordance with his physician's advice, who stated that a voyage across the Atlantic, and a residence of some months in a semi-Tropical latitude, might entirely re-establish his health. The change, however, did not benefit him, for he died three months after his arrival. The choice was then presented to Miss Goodwin of remaining with her brother's family, or of returning to England with her stepmother. She chose the former ; and thus it happened that the poet was often thrown into her society.

On the 12th of January, 1864, our poet came to the State Capital, prepared to assume his duties as editor, and in little more than a month, that is to say, on the 16th of the ensuing February, he married Miss Goodwin, taking his bride to a humble home, but one glorified, I venture to say, by anticipations as bright, pure, and ardent as ever flushed the fancy and elevated the heart of the richest and most prosperous of bridegrooms.

It is pleasant to dwell upon his honeymoon, and the few months immediately succeeding it; to picture his cheerful walks from his home to the office, and from the office to his home again. He proved himself a judicious and able editor, and his industry never flagged.

Once or twice during these comparatively halcyon days,

I received affectionate letters from him; but amid his in-
cessant occupations he could do no more than give me an
outline of his employments, prospects, and occasional business
annoyances, which latter, however, as I gathered from his
tone, were never permitted to ruffle his serene domestic
atmosphere. "All the poetry in my nature," wrote he,
"has been fagged out of me, I fear! I work very hard.
Besides writing the 'leaders' of the paper, I often descend,
as you may have noticed, into the local columns. My purpose is to show that a poet can *drudge* as well as a duller
man, and therefore I don't complain! But, O God! for
leisure enough to breathe, although at rarest intervals, the
air of the Aonian mount! By the way," he inquires in the
same note, "What think you of the War? Shall we
ever see its end, favorable or unfavorable, glorious or fatal?
Its end, deuce take me! but I sometimes fear it has been
like the end of the Irishman's rope—cut off!"

Another end, at least, was imminent, the end of his own
hard-won quiet; his independence and partial prosperity.

But just on the verge of the catastrophe, an intense joy
was granted him. Upon Christmas Eve, 1864, his son
WILLIE was born!—a child of unusual promise, and of a
beauty described as exquisite.

In a communication all *couleur de rose*, bubbling over with
pride and delight, he says, "At length, my dear P——, we
stand upon the same height of paternity—quite a celestial
elevation to me! If you could only see my boy! Everybody
wonders at him! He is so transparently fair; so ethereal!"

A few weeks of dalliance with his infant beauty; of un-
disturbed calm in the little nest of a home he had reared for
himself and his wife, and then came fearful reports of inva-
sion; the rapid, overwhelming march of the enemy, and
upon the 17th of February, 1865 (just one year *and a day*,

since Timrod's marriage), the devoted city of Columbia was given up to the mercies of Sherman and his troops.

What followed is known to all—the conflagration, the sack, the universal terror and despair! As one whose vigorous, patriotic editorials had made him obnoxious to Federal vengeance, Timrod was forced, while this foreign army occupied the town, to remain concealed. When they left, he rejoined his anxious "womankind," to behold, in common with thousands of others, such a scene of desolation as mortal eyes have seldom dwelt upon.

An imperfect glimpse of his condition; of what he did and suffered for the next twelvemonth, may be obtained from this letter, addressed to me, and dated "*Columbia, March* 30*th*, 1866:

"My dear P——: Nothing has come to me for the past year which has given me such pleasure as your letter of the —— instant. I am overjoyed to renew our correspondence.

"Dear old fellow! heart and hand, body, soul, and spirit, I am still yours!

"I have the right poet's inclination to plunge *in medias res.* You ask me to tell you my story for the last year. I can embody it all in a few words: *beggary, starvation, death,* * *bitter grief, utter want of hope!* But let me be a little more particular, that you may learn where I stand. You know, I suppose, that the Sherman raid destroyed my business. Since that time I have been residing with my sister, Mrs. Goodwin. Both my sister and myself are completely impoverished. We have lived for a long period, and are still living, on the proceeds of the gradual sale of furniture and plate. We have—

---

* Five months before, on the 23d of October, 1865, Timrod's idolized child was taken from him. He died somewhat suddenly. In that little grave, a large portion of the father's heart was buried. The poet was never quite his old self again.

let me see!—yes, we have eaten two silver pitchers, one or two dozen silver forks, several sofas, innumerable chairs, and a huge —— bedstead!!

" Until December, I had no employment. Mr. —— passed through Columbia in November on his way to the sea-board. He called on me, informed me that he was going to re-establish his paper in Charleston, and promised that I should have my old interest in it.

"On reaching Charleston, he started ' *The Carolinian*,' and soon he wrote me (but addressing me as a mere *employé*), and offering a salary of fifteen dollars a week for daily editorials. Necessity compelled me to accept this offer.

" I have now hacked on for *four* months, and as yet have failed to receive a single month's pay.

" The plain truth is, Mr. —— *can't* pay ! He made a grave mistake in carrying his paper to Charleston. Under the shadow of the ' *News*' and ' *Courier*,' it is languishing, and must die ! What I am going to do, I can't imagine.

"As for supporting myself and a large family—wife, mother, sister and nieces, by *literary* work—'tis utterly preposterous!

" In a ' forlorn-hope ' sort of mood, and as a mere experiment, I forwarded some poems in my best style to certain Northern periodicals, and in every instance they were coldly declined.

" So all hope of thus turning my rhymes into bread must be resigned." Whereupon, with a self-mocking *spurt* of humor, he adds, " Little Jack Horner, who sang for his supper, and got his plum cake, was a far more lucky minstrel than I am! * * * To confess the truth, my dear P——, I not only feel that I can write no more verse, but I am perfectly indifferent to the fate of what I have already composed.

"I would consign every line of it to eternal oblivion, for —*one hundred dollars in hand!* * * * * *

"I can tell you nothing about Charleston, although in February, having a free Railroad ticket, I went down and spent three days there. My eyes were blind to everything and everybody but a few old friends. I dined with Bruns; had a night of it at Henry Raymond's, and went to see the lions in the circus!

"The sum of this small experience of my native town is, that the people are generally impoverished, suffering, despondent, with all the spring and elasticity taken out of them. * * * * My wife has been very sick. Her low condition of health, indeed, makes me continually anxious."

A fair conception of Timrod's editorial style—its picturesqueness and beauty, allied to much quiet power, may be obtained by a perusal of *three* brief articles of his, published in "*The Carolinian.*"

The first of these, evidently composed during the closing days of the war, is called

"THE ALABAMA."

"The bones of the noble 'Alabama,' full fathom five under the English channel, have, perchance, long ere this, suffered 'a sea change into something rich and strange.' Precious jewels these bones would be if they could be fished up now —yet not, thank Heaven, of that sort of value which would make our Destructive friends think it worth while to bring them into the Admiralty courts. A Southron might possibly be permitted to treasure a shell-covered rib, without fear of having it torn from him by the myrmidons of the law. And well might that Southron—well indeed might the citizen of any section of the United States, if he would consider the matter magnanimously—cherish any relic that could be recovered of this dead lioness of the seas. For what a wonderful history was hers! A single ship matched against one

of the mightiest navies of the world, yet keeping the ocean
in defiance of all pursuit for—we forget—how many years!
Flitting like a phantom across the waters, appearing at aston-
ishingly short intervals in the most opposite quarters of the
globe, we used to follow her track with something of that
weird interest which was wont to thrill us in our boyhood
when poring over a tale of the ghostly Dutchman of the
Cape.   At one time lost in the fogs of the Northern Atlantic,
at another popping up in the region of the trade winds, scat-
tering dismay among the clippers; and anon, far away in the
direction of the dawn, where much more precious spoil might
be reaped, or, if not reaped, then consigned to that vast locker
of which the mythic ' Davy' of the sailor, is said to keep
the key—such were the reports that reached us from month
to month of this almost ubiquitous vessel.   Now we heard,
perhaps, that, in the neighborhood of the Golden Cher-
sonesus, or under the rich shores of that ' utmost Indian isle
Toprobane,' some homeward-bound Englishman had been
startled by the dull boom of guns across the billows, while a
red light upon the horizon informed him that the ' Alabama'
was illuminating those remote seas with the fires of Confederate revenge; and, again a little later, it was bruited from
port to port that she was speeding across the main—haply
amazing the gentle islanders of the Pacific with the gleam
of her beautiful but unfamiliar flag—to complete the circuit
of her awful mission with the destruction of a few treasure
ships of the Ophir of the West!   The repeated achievement
of the adventure has rendered the circumnavigation of the
globe in these modern days a commonplace thing; but there
was that in the errand upon which the ' Alabama' was
bound, which reinvested the voyage with its old romance; so
that, in accompanying the Southern cruiser upon her various
paths, we used to experience a feeling somewhat resembling

that imaginative one which WORDSWORTH has expressed in these deep-toned lines:

‘ Almost as it was when ships were rare,
From time to time, like pilgrims, here and there,
Crossing the waters, doubt and something dark,
Of the old sea some reverential fear,
Were with us as we watched thee, noble bark.’

"The career of the ‘ Alabama’ was worthily closed. Challenged by a foe more powerful than herself, she sallied forth bravely to battle and went down in the sight of the coast of one people and of the ships of another, who each knew how to admire the valor which she had displayed. What a pity and what a wonder it is that the same generous appreciation of her glorious story, and its not less glorious end, is not shared in the country which enshrines the name of LAWRENCE! Who could believe, that did not know it, that we Southrons are expected by those who call us brethren to remember this gallant ship only as a corsair, and its venerated commander as a pirate."

The *two* others, written at a later date, some months in fact after the surrender at Appomattox, are certainly fine specimens of "poetic prose."

" SPRING'S LESSONS."

"Spring, thank Heaven, is not subject to radical rule, or pregnable to radical intrigues; otherwise, she would certainly be proscribed, outlawed or expatriated by Thaddeus Stevens and his crew. For Spring is a true reconstructionist—a reconstructionist in the best and most practical sense. There is not a nook in the land in which she is not at this moment exerting her influence, in preparing a way for the restoration of the South. No politician may oppose her; her power defies embarrassment; but she is not altogether independent

of help.   She brings us balmy airs and gentle dews, golden
suns and silver rains; and she says to us: 'These are the
materials of the only work in which you need be at present
concerned: avail yourselves of them to re-clothe your naked
country and feed your impoverished people, and you will find
that, in the discharge of that task, you have taken the course
which will most certainly and most peacefully conduct you
to the position which you desire.   Turn not aside to bandy
epithets with your enemies; stuff your ears like the princess
in the 'Arabian Nights,' against words of insult and wrong;
pause not to muse over your condition, or to question your
prospects; but toil on bravely, silently, surely, and you
will reap a reward to which the yellow water, talking bird,
and the singing tree of the fairy tale, are not to be compared.'

"Such are the words of wise and kindly counsel, which, if
we attend rightly, we may all hear in the winds and read in
the skies of spring.   Nowhere, however, does she speak with
so eloquent a voice or so pathetic an effect as in this ruined
town.*   She covers our devastated courts with images of reno-
vation in the shape of flowers; she hangs once more in our
blasted gardens the fragrant lamps of the jessamine; in the
streets, she kindles the maple like a beacon announcing
peace; and from amidst the charred and blackened ruins of
once happy homes, she pours through the mouth of her
favorite musician, the mocking-bird, a song of hope and joy.
What is the lesson which she designs by these means to convey?   It may be summed in a single sentence—forgetfulness
of the past, effort in the present, and trust for the future!"

"NAMES OF THE MONTHS PHONETICALLY EX-PRESSIVE."

"Talking of the offices of March and April, reminds us of
a fancy of ours which we desire to record.   It will, however,

---

* Columbia, S. C.

find no sympathy from those who read words with the eye, or hear them with the ear alone. We speak only to the rare few who possess an inner sense of which the common world knows nothing. The fancy is that each month has a name phonetically expressive (to their inner sense, mark you) of its character. For example, the winds seem to us to rumble in the word *March* as audibly as they did in the cave of Æolus. *April* falls from the tongue like silver rain. What name but *May* could be fitly given to that beautiful, blue-eyed, and exquisitely feminine month? *June*, sounded with the proper depth of tone, is exactly like the humming of bees. The wings of millions of insects and the rustle of innumerable leaves may be found in the words *July* and *August*. *September* whistles through more than its initial letter like an autumnal gale. *October* has a royal sound, that fills the mouth like Napoleon or Plantagenet. It is a name worthy of that imperial month, whose gorgeous sunsets and magnificent woods indicate its supremacy both in earth and sky. We have Burns' authority for asserting that ' *November* chill blows loud with angry sough.' Lastly, he to whom the mere syllables of December, January and February do not suggest all that belongs to Winter—its cheerful firesides as well as its ice and snow—lacks the organ we address.

" With this fancy in our head, we often wonder how those people feel who leave this country or England for the South Temperate zone. Surely, when they ' see roses in December, ice in June,' they must undergo a moral sensation equivalent to the bodily one produced by standing on one's head."

In the winter of 1866 I again heard from him.

" COLUMBIA, *Nov.* 19*th*, 1866.

" MY DEAR P—— :—Your letter found me a scribe in the

Governor's Office, where I work every day from 9 A.M. to 7 P.M. I snatch a moment from my labor to answer your note. Yes; I have had a sad and hard struggle of it for the past six months, but just as I was about to despair of help from God or man, I received from Governor Orr a temporary appointment as an assistant secretary, or rather, clerk. The appointment is but for a month or so, in order to get through a certain amount of work which crowds upon the department at this time. It ensures me, however, *a month's supply of bread and bacon ;* that devoured, I'll trust in God that something else will turn up. This last is no conventional remark. I am really learning, P——, *to trust in God !*

"My health is very wretched. The doctors prescribe change of air, but, of course, that remedy is impossible at present. Both on this account, and to shake hands once more with you, old friend and true heart, I should like to accept the invitation to your home.

"But here I must stay like a lugubrious fowl, to scratch for corn. I shall, however, keep your invitation in memory, and as soon as practicable, be assured, I will gladly take a turn or two upon your cot in the country.

"You say nothing about Mrs. H——, and your boy, Willie! Ah, how ineffably dear *that name* has become to me now. He (my own lost Willie) was the sweetest child. But every body thought him too ethereal to live, even when he seemed in the most perfect health !"

In the January of 1867, Timrod, addressing his friend, Judge Bryan, says: "My term of service in the Executive office ended at the close of the session. It was no child's play. On *two* occasions I wrote *from* 10 *o'clock one morning until the sunrise of the next day* (a brief intermission for dinner being allowed).

"A laborious life, yet not half so laborious, after all, as having nothing to do!

" The wages of the office I held barely sufficed to feed our family. We had still to depend upon the sale of furniture and plate for *rent*. On the 24th we must perforce leave the house we now occupy. *I'm looking for a small hole to squeeze ourselves in !* "

A flitting glimpse of hope had, some months before, beguiled him in the shape of an invitation from the publisher, Mr. Richardson, then on a visit to the South, to leave his home troubles awhile, and to become his (Mr. R.'s) guest in New York city. Something, too, was rather vaguely said of the Publisher's willingness to undertake an edition of a few of Timrod's selected poems; but the chronic impecuniosity of the latter made void the whole plan as soon almost as conceived. I can never cease to regret this; for had Timrod made the personal acquaintance of some among the New York and Boston *Literati*, it is quite possible that his fate would have been wholly different. Such high-hearted men as Bryant, Whipple, Holmes, and Whittier, would have recognized equally the genius of the man, and his modest worth and purity of temperament. Some beneficent suggestion, some practical help might have reached him from them; since the fact that in a special sense he was the poet of his section, could have weighed in their estimation but little against the claims of his intellect, his character, and, I may add, his undeserved misfortunes. * * *

In the April of 1867 I received a note from my friend in which he says that my long-standing invitation to the country would soon be answered by him personally. " Our watchful Doctor," he proceeds, "has been urging me more persistently than ever to change the air. I shall obey him. You tempt me, dear P——, not only with your light, bracing, aromatic pine-land atmosphere—the very thing I need—and with the happy prospect of your own society, but you speak of the publishers sending you their *new books!* You can afford to put up with what Mr. Simms really appears to consider appetizing fare, so unctuously does he refer to it (I mean 'hog and hominy') if, mean time, instead of having your imagination starved, it (or she ?) is free to wander in fresh literary pastures.

"*Apropos* of literature and rhymsters, I have lately had a *modest* request preferred me by a committee of Richmond ladies, intent upon establishing a Bazaar, or something, in that city. It was, to write within a fortnight, a poem on the history of 'Fort Sumter,' beginning with the shot at the 'STAR OF THE WEST,' and ending with the elevation of the United States flag over the ruins of the Fort!! This poem I was further requested to make long enough to fill *eighty printed octavo pages*, or—it was obligingly qualified—less!! Need I say that I respectfully declined to undertake the task?"

In less than a week the poet himself had followed his letter. He found me with my family, established in a crazy wooden shanty, dignified as a cottage, near the track of the main Georgia Railroad, and about sixteen miles from Augusta. Our little apology for a dwelling was perched on the top of a hill, overlooking in several directions hundreds of leagues of pine-barren; there were, as yet, neither garden nor enclosure near it, and a wilder, more desolate, and savage-looking home, could hardly have been seen east of the great prairies. Hither, so to speak, had the eruption of war hurled us; for our old residence on the beautiful Carolina coast had been destroyed by fire; the State of our nativity was a blackened, smoking ruin, and we were consequently grateful for *any* shelter, however lowly, in which

it was possible to live at peace and *in freedom!* Human
hearts can be as warm in a shanty, with leaking roof and
shutterless windows, as in the palace of the Doges, and in
the enthusiasm of the poet's welcome we strove to make
amends for the general poverty of his accommodations, and
a very perceptible coarseness of the *cuisine.* But he, poor
fellow, had. been the victim of privations so much worse,
that he cared for none of these things, or rather, he pro-
fessed (with frequent deep-drawn sighs of relief), to be perfectly content in the mere consciousness of present freedom
from anxiety.

A month's sojourn in our Robinson Crusoe solitude greatly
improved both his strength and spirits. Leisure, saunter-
ings through the great balmy pine forest, luxurious explora-
tions of shadowy glens and valleys, full of exquisite varieties
of wild flowers; the warm, dry, delicious climate which in-
vited him to take his *dolce far niente* under the boughs of
murmuring trees, outstretched upon a couch of brown pine-
needles, as elastic as it was odorous, all promised to bring
back his poetical enthusiasm, and to set in genial motion the
half frozen springs of his invention and fancy. But his
term of holiday was too limited.

Circumstances compelled his return to the capital, and
there the old, terrible, destructive life of *want* recommenced.
For let it be distinctly and finally understood, that in alluding to Timrod's *poverty* I do *not* mean the factitious poverty
of your well-to-do ingrate, whether epicure or *gourmand,*
who, in the midst of substantial plenty, whimpers over a
lost paradise of venison, French *patés,* and champagne, *but
that frequent actual lack of food, those grim encounters with starvation,* which sap the life, chill the heart-blood, madden the
brain!   *   *   *   *   *   *   *

*   *   * In the latter summer-tide of this same year, I

again persuaded him to visit me. Ah! how sacred now, how sad and sweet are the memories of that rich, clear, prodigal August of '67!

We would rest on the hill-sides, in the swaying golden shadows, watching together the Titanic masses of snow-white clouds which floated slowly and vaguely through the sky, suggesting by their form, whiteness, and serene motion, despite the season, flotillas of icebergs upon Arctic seas. Like *lazzaroni* we basked in the quiet noons, sunk into depths on depths of reverie, or perhaps of yet more "charm-éd sleep." Or we smoked, conversing lazily between the puffs,

> " Next to some pine whose antique roots just peeped
> From out the crumbling bases of the sand."

But the evenings, with their gorgeous sunsets "rolling down like a chorus," and the "gray-eyed melancholy gloam-ing," were the favorite hours of the day with him. He would often apostrophize twilight in the language of Words-worth's sonnet:

> " Hail, twilight! sovereign of one peaceful hour!
> Not dull art thou as undiscerning night;
> But only studious to remove from sight
> Day's mutable distinctions."

" Yes," said he, " she is indeed the sovereign *of one peace-ful hour!* In the hardest, busiest time, one feels the calm, merciful-minded queen stealing upon one in the fading light, and 'whispering,' as Ford has it (or is it Fletcher ?) '*whis-pering* tranquility!'"

When in-doors, and disposed to read, he took much pleasure in perusing the poems of Robert Buchanan and Miss Ingelow. The latter's *Ballads* particularly delighted him.

One, written "in the old English manner," he quickly learned by heart, repeating it with a relish and fervor indescribable.

Here is the opening stanza:

"Come out and hear the waters shoot, the owlet hoot, the
    owlet hoot;
Yon crescent moon, a golden boat, hangs dim behind the
    tree, O!
The dropping thorn makes white the grass, O! sweetest lass,
    and sweetest lass
Come out and smell the ricks of hay adown the croft with
    me, O!"

With but a slight effort of memory I can vividly recall his voice and manner in repeating these simple yet beautiful lines.

They were the last verses I ever heard from the poet's lips.

Just as the woods were assuming their first delicate autumnal tints, Timrod took his leave of us. In a conversation on the night but one previous to his departure, we had been speaking of Dr. Parr and other literary persons of unusual age, when he observed: "I hav'nt the slightest desire, P——, to be an octogenarian, far less a centenarian, like old Parr; but I DO hope that I may be spared until I am *fifty* or fifty-five."

"About Shakespeare's age," I suggested.

"Oh!" he replied, smiling, "I was not thinking of THAT; but I'm sure that after fifty-five I would begin to wither, mind and body, and one hates the idea of a mummy, intellectual or physical. Do you remember that picture of extreme old age which Charles Reade gives us in '*Never too Late to Mend?*' George Fielding, the hero, is about going away

from England to try his luck in Australia. All his friends
and relations are around him, expressing their sorrow at his
enforced voyage; all but his grandfather, aged ninety-two,
who sits stolid and mumbling in his arm-chair.

" 'Grandfather!' shouts George into the deafened ears,
'I'm going a long journey; mayhap, shall never see you
again; speak a word to me before I go!' Grandfather looks
up, brightens for a moment, and cackles feebly out, 'George,
fetch me some *snuff* from where you're going. See now
(half whimpering), I'm out of snuff.' A good point in the
way of illustration, but not a pleasant picture."

On the 13th of September, ten days after Timrod's return
to Columbia, he wrote me the following note:

"DEAR P——: I have been too sick to write before, and
am still too sick to drop you more than a few lines. You
will be surprised and pained to hear that I have had a severe
hemorrhage of the lungs. It came upon me without a
moment's warning, my mouth being filled with blood while
I was listening to Wm. Talley talking.

"I did not come home an instant too soon. I found them
without money or provisions.* Fortunately, I brought with
me a small sum—I won't tell you how small—but six dollars of it was from the editor of the ' *Opinion*,' for my last
poem. * * *

"I left your climate to my injury. But not only for the

* When one thinks how little—how *very* little of the " world's
gear" would have served to make this most unexacting of mortals
content, nay, happy! there is something in the dogged persist-
ence and cruel energy of the fate which harassed and wounded
him along almost every yard of his rugged life-path, that resem-
bled the virulence of a Greek Nemesis, rather than the chastenings
of a benignant Providence.

sake of my health, I begin already to look back with longing regret to 'Copse Hill.' You have all made me feel as if I had *two* beloved homes!

"I wish that I could divide myself between them; or that I had wings, so that I might flit from one to other in a moment.

"I hope soon to write you at length. Yours, etc."

Again on the 16th I heard from him, thus:

"Yesterday I had a still more copious hemorrhage! It occurred in the street—the blood came in jets from my mouth; you might have tracked me home in crimson!

"I am lying supine in bed, forbidden to speak, or make any exertion whatever. But I can't resist the temptation of dropping you a line, in the hope of calling forth a score or two from you in return.

"An awkward time this for me to be sick! We are destitute of funds, almost of food. But God will provide!

" I send you a *Sonnet*, written the other day, as an Obituary for Mr. Harris Simons. Tell me what you think of it—be sure! Love to your mother, wife, and my precious Willie" (since the death of his own child, he had turned with a yearning affection to my boy). "Let me hear from you soon —*very* soon! You'll do me more good than medicines!" etc.

The *Sonnet* he mentions is here before me, written in pencil on a scant fragment of paper, but in a calligraphy clear and bold as ever:

IN MEMORIAM—HARRIS SIMONS.

" True Christian, tender husband, gentle sire,
   A stricken household mourns thee, but its loss
   Is Heaven's gain and thine; upon the cross

> God hangs the crown, the pinion, and the lyre;
> And thou hast won them all.　Could we desire
> 　To quench that diadem's celestial light ;
> 　To hush thy song and stay thy heavenward flight,
> Because we miss thee by this autumn fire ?
> Ah, no ! ah, no !—chant on !—soar on !—reign on !
> 　For we are better—thou art happier thus !
> And haply from the splendor of thy throne,
> 　Or haply from the echoes of thy psalm,
> 　Something may fall upon us, like the calm
> To which thou shalt hereafter welcome us ! "

Reading these lines, no shadow of a presentiment oppressed me.　I simply admired the art of the Sonnet, and its tender Christian feeling, unconscious that another " In Memoriam " would soon be called for, steeped in the bitterness of an irremediable grief !

On the 25th of the month this confidence in Timrod's recovery was confirmed by a letter from Mrs. Goodwin.

" Our brother," she writes, " is *decidedly better ;* and if there be no recurrence of the hemorrhage, will, I hope, be soon convalescent ! "

A week and upwards passed on in silence.　I received no more communications from Columbia.　But early in October a vaguely threatening report reached my ears.　On the 9th it was mournfully confirmed.　Forty-eight hours before, Henry Timrod had expired !

The circumstances attendant upon his last illness and death, are related by his sister in terms at once so graphically minute, and so tenderly pathetic, that I cannot but feel justified in laying the letter—although a private one—before my readers.

> " Alas ! alas ! in every tremulous line
> We see but heartbreak and the touch of tears ! "

"Columbia, *October* 22*d*, 1867.

"My Dear Friend:

"You are, I know, anxiously awaiting the particulars of *those* last sad days!

"Painful as the effort is, I feel that to you, his dearest friend, I ought *at once* to write.

"You will remember that my last letter was scarcely as hopeful as the former had been.* Hal's apprehension of another hemorrhage seemed to increase. Each cough he gave, I saw the look of uneasiness on his face, and each cough sent a thrill of terror to my heart!

" The idea that he was to *choke* to death by a sudden rush of blood from the lungs, haunted him like a spectre ; no persuasions could induce him to believe that there was really no danger.

" His fears, alas! proved but too sure premonitions of the truth. On Wednesday morning (2d of October), at two o'clock, I was roused to witness once more the life stream flowing from his lips, while every instant respiration became more difficult.

" The hemorrhage, however, was soon checked, but its effect on his *nervous system* was fatal! He never rallied again!

" Doctors Gibbes and Talley spent hours by his bedside, endeavoring by every human means to arrest the progress of the disease; but pneumonic symptoms made their appearance, and hope was gone!

" On Friday morning Dr. Gibbes said, 'Mr. Timrod, I think it my duty to tell you that I can see no chance of your recovery!' Never shall I forget the fearfully startled expression of my brother's face at this announcement. After

---

* This note miscarried.

the Doctor went, he said to me, 'And is *this* to be the end
of all—so soon! so soon! and I have achieved so little ! I
thought to have done so much! I had just before my first
attack fallen into a strain of such pure and delicate fancies.
I do think this winter I would have done more than I have ever
done; yes, I should have written more purely, and with a
greater delicacy. And then I have loved you all so much!
Oh! how *can* I leave you?'

"A little while after he said, 'Do you not think I could
will to live ?' adding with a smile, 'I might make an effort,
like Mrs. Dombey, you know!'

"And indeed, so resolutely did he seem to combat with
the powers of Death, that the rest of that day (Friday) he
appeared to grow stronger, and the symptoms were more
favorable; so much more so, in fact, that both physicians, at
night, pronounced a change for the better.

"Captain Hugh Thompson sat up with him that night, I
bearing him company. He begged us to talk, saying he liked
to hear our voices; and in the morning observed, 'I have
enjoyed this night; I slept when I wanted, and listened when
I liked.'

"I must not omit to say, that from the first serious hemorrhage his mind turned to religious subjects, and that the New
Testament was always near his pillow. He would every now
and then ask me to read a chapter from the Gospels, and to
pray with him.

"On Saturday morning he seemed cheerful, and even san-
guine; but in the afternoon the great pain in his side, and
difficulty of breathing, returned. He requested the subcu-
taneous injection of a portion of morphine. This had given
him relief several times before. It was done, and he fell into
a gentle sleep.

"I sat up with him again, intending to call his wife to

take my place at two o'clock; but at *two* he awoke, and O! God! *that* awakening!

"It was the commencement of the last struggle. The strongest convulsions shook his already worn-out frame. To listen to those groans—those shrieks, was unutterable horror!—was agony untold! For hours the struggle lasted, and then came for a space partial quiet and consciousness. He knew that he was dying. 'Oh!' I murmured to him, 'you will soon be at rest now.' 'Yes,' he replied, in a tone so mournful, it seemed the wail of a life-time of desolation; 'yes, my sister, *but love is sweeter than rest!*'

"In the early hush of that Sabbath morning, he for the first time commemorated the love and sufferings of our ascended Lord; the Holy Communion having been administered to him by a clergyman of our church.

"Most strange, solemn, and sad was the sight to those who stood about his death-bed. He looked upon the struggle of life and death as if from the position of an earnest but outside observer. Once he said, 'And so THIS is Death! the struggle has come at last. It is curious to watch it. It appears like two tides—two tides advancing and retreating, these powers of Life and Death! Now the power of Death recedes; but wait, it will advance again triumphant.' Then, with a look of eager, yet hushed expectation, he seemed to watch the conflict.

"Again he said, 'So this is Death! how strange! were I a metaphysician I would analyze it; but as it is, I can only watch.'

"Words fail to describe the awful solemnity with which these dying words of the poet impressed all who heard him. Everybody was in tears.

"Once, turning to me, he asked, 'Do you remember that little poem of mine?

    ' " Somewhere on this earthly planet
      In the dust of flowers to be,
      In the dew-drop and the sunshine
      Waits a solemn hour for me." '

    " ' Yes,' I replied, ' and now that hour, which then seemed so far away, has come.'

    " Often he would fold his arms, and repeat two lines of his favorite hymn:

      ' Jesus, lover of my soul,' etc.

    " At every conscious interval his prayers to our atoning Lord were unceasing.

    " During·the earlier part of the last night he slept for many hours. Awaking, he missed me, and asked that I should be called. On my going to him, he said, ' Well, Emily, I am really dying now, but my trust is in Christ.' Then quoting those lines of Milton, ' *Death rides triumphant,*' etc., he added, ' Oh, may I be able to say, thanks be to God who giveth us the victory through our Lord Jesus Christ.'

    " An unquenchable *thirst* consumed him. Nothing could allay that dreadful torture. He whispered, as I placed the water to his lips, ' Don't you remember that passage I once quoted to you from " King John?" I had always such a horror of quenchless thirst, and now I suffer it!' He alluded to the passage—

      " And none of you will let the Winter come,
        To thrust his icy fingers in my maw !"

    " Just a day or two before he left on a visit to you at ' Copse Hill,' in one of our evening rambles he had repeated the passage to me with a remark on the extraordinary force of the words.

"Katie took my place by him at 5 o'clock (in the morning), and never again left his side. The last spoonful of water she gave him, he could not swallow. 'Never mind,' he said, 'I shall soon drink of the river of Eternal Life.'

" Shortly after he slept peacefully in Christ.

"He died at the *very hour* which, years ago, he had predicted would be his death-hour. The whisper, '*He is gone!*' went forth as '*day purpled in the zenith!*'" etc., etc.

On the —— of October, the mortal remains of the poet, so worn and shattered, were buried in the cemetery of Trinity Church, Columbia.

There, in the ruined capital of his native State, whence scholarship, culture, and social purity have been banished to give place to the orgies of semi-barbarians and the political trickery of adventurers and traitors,—there, tranquil amid the vulgar turmoil of factions, reposes the dust of one of the truest and sweetest singers this country has given to the world.

Nature, kinder to his senseless ashes than ever Fortune had been to the living man, is prodigal around his grave— unmarked and unrecorded though it be—of her flowers and verdant grasses, of her rains that fertilize, and her purifying dews. The peace he loved, and so vainly longed for through stormy years, has crept to him at last, but only to fall upon the pallid eyelids, closed forever—upon the pulseless limbs and the breathless, broken heart! Still it is good to know that—

" After life's fitful fever, he sleeps well."

Yet, from this mere material repose, this quiet of decaying atoms, surely the most sceptical of thinkers, in contemplation of *such* a life, and *such* a death, must instinctively look

from earth to heaven; from the bruised and mouldering clod
to the spirit infinitely exalted, and radiant in redemption,

" A calm, a beautiful, a sacred star,"

thus imagining, and perchance believing, though it be but
for an hour, in the mysterious ameliorations of eternity!

*   *   *   *   *   *   *   *

Were one to sum up the idiosyncrasies of Timrod's genius
and poetic manner, I think it would be just to notice in the
first place, the simplicity, clearness, purity, and straight-
forward force of his imagination, which within its appointed
bounds (and these limitations are as strictly marked as its
vivid capabilities themselves) is always a true enchanter,
not owning the slightest relation to that mechanical faculty,
so commonly confounded with imagination, which, instead
of evolving its material out of the heart of its own electric
being, is content to work *from without*, piling up a tedious cat-
alogue of qualities, whether its attempts be directed towards
description merely, or towards the subtleties of spiritual
analysis. Thus it happens that Timrod's productions carry
with them always "a firm body of thought." They do not
appeal, like too many of Edgar Poe's, to our sense of rhythmic
harmony *alone;* nor are they charming, but mystic utter-
ances, which here and there may strike a vaguely solemn
echo in the heart of the visionary dreamer.

No! beneath the surface of his delicate imagery, and
rhythmic sweetness of numbers, rest deeply imbedded the
"golden ores of wisdom."

As an artist, he fulfilled one of Coleridge's many definitions
of poetry ("the best words in the best order"), with a tact
as exquisite as it was unerring. *And his style is literally himself!* "It has the form, and follows the movement of his

nature, and is shaped into the expression of the exact mood, sentiment, or thought out of which the poem springs. Therefore his compositions—with all their elegance, finish, and superb propriety of diction—always leave the impression of having been *born*, not manufactured or made."

His *morale* is perfect. What can speak more emphatically for the native soundness, wholesomeness, and untainted virility of his genius, than the absence from his works of all morbid arraignments of the Eternal justice or mercy ; all blasphemous hardihood and whining complaint—in a word, all *Byronism* of sentiment, despite the ceaseless trials of his individual experience, his sorrows, humiliations, and corroding want.

While other poets, "the curled darlings of Fortune," were, like Master Stephen, deliberately procuring "stools to be melancholy upon," ostentatiously showing themselves "sad as Night for very wantonness," he whose pains were only too real, into whose soul the iron had deeply entered, could forget himself in his divine art, and sing for us many a strain as fresh and breezy as the west wind "laden with woodland fragrance," as healthfully inspiriting as the breath of a May morning!

There were likewise in his intellect and temperament, to appear occasionally in his verses, a certain arch, Ariel-like humor and delightful playfulness of fancy. His little poem of "*Baby's Age*," his "*Præceptor Amat*," etc., indicate a vein of sentiment genial, sportive and airy, that might, under favorable auspices, have been developed into many kindred pieces of a gay fanciful humor, calculated to relieve the pervading earnestness of his general style of composition and reflection.

I cannot more fitly close this imperfect sketch, than with Dr. Bruns' graphic description of Timrod's personal appearance, and of some prominent traits of his social character:

" In stature," he says, " Timrod was far below the medium height. He had always excelled in boyish sports, and as he grew to manhood, his unusual breadth of shoulder still seemed to indicate a physical vigor which the slender wrists, thin, transparent hands, and habitually lax attitude, but too plainly contradicted.

" The square jaw was almost stern in its strongly pronounced lines, the mouth large, the lips exquisitely sensitive, the gray eyes set deeply under massive brows, and full of a melancholy and pleading tenderness, which attracted attention to his face at once, as the face of one who had thought and suffered much.

" His walk was quick and nervous, with an energy in it that betokened decision of character, but illy sustained by the stammering speech; for in society he was the shyest and most undemonstrative of men. To a *single* friend whom he trusted, he would pour out his inmost heart; but let two or three be gathered together, above all, introduce a stranger, and he instantly became a quiet, unobtrusive listener, though never a moody, or uncongenial one!

" Among men of letters, he was always esteemed as a most sympathetic companion; timid, reserved, unready if taken by surprise, but highly cultivated, and still more highly endowed.

" The key to his social character was to be found in the feminine gentleness of his temperament. He shrank from noisy debate, and the wordy clash of argument, as from a blow! It stunned and bewildered him, and left him in the *mêlée* alike incapable of defence or attack. And yet, when some burly protagonist would thrust himself too rudely into the ring, and try to bear down opposition by sheer vehemence of declamation, from the corner where he sat ensconced in unregarded silence, *he would suddenly sling out some sharp, swift pebble of thought*, which he had been slowly rounding, and smite with an aim so keen and true as rarely failed to bring down the boastful Anakim ! "

DEDICATION.

TO K. S. G.

Fair Saxon, in my lover's creed,
My love were smaller than your meed,
And you might justly deem it slight,
As wanting truth as well as sight,
If, in that image which is shrined
Where thoughts are sacred, you could find
A single charm, or more or less,
Than you to all kind eyes possess.
To me, even in the happiest dreams,
Where, flushed with love's just dawning gleams,
My hopes their radiant wings unfurl,
You're but a simple English girl,
No fairer, grace for grace arrayed,
Than many a simple Southern maid;
With faults enough to make the good
Seem sweeter far than else it would;
Frank in your anger and your glee,
And true as English natures be,
Yet not without some maiden art
Which hides a loving English heart.

Still there are moments, brief and bright,
When fancy, by a poet's light,

Beholds you clothed with loftier charms
Than love e'er gave to mortal arms.
A spell is woven on the air
From your brown eyes and golden hair,
And all at once you seem to stand
Before me as your native land,
With all her greatness in your guise,
And all her glory in your eyes;
And sometimes, as if angels sung,
I hear her poets on your tongue.
And, therefore, I, who from a boy
Have felt an almost English joy
In England's undecaying might,
And England's love of truth and right,
Next to my own young country's fame
Holding her honor and her name,
I—who, though born where not a vale
Hath ever nursed a nightingale,
Have fed my muse with English song
Until her feeble wing grew strong—
Feel, while with all the reverence meet
I lay this volume at your feet,
As if through your dear self I pay,
For many a deep and deathless lay,
For noble lessons nobly taught,
For tears, for laughter, and for thought,
A portion of the mighty debt
We owe to Shakespeare's England yet!

Poems of Henry Timrod.

KATIE.

It may be through some foreign grace,
And unfamiliar charm of face;
It may be that across the foam
Which bore her from her childhood's home,
By some strange spell, my Katie brought,
Along with English creeds and thought—
Entangled in her golden hair—
Some English sunshine, warmth, and air!
I cannot tell—but here to-day,
A thousand billowy leagues away
From that green isle whose twilight skies
No darker are than Katie's eyes,
She seems to me, go where she will,
An English girl in England still!

I meet her on the dusty street,
And daisies spring about her feet;
Or, touched to life beneath her tread,
An English cowslip lifts its head;
And, as to do her grace, rise up
The primrose and the buttercup!

4

1 roam with her through fields of cane,
And seem to stroll an English lane,
Which, white with blossoms of the May,
Spreads its green carpet in her way!
As fancy wills, the path beneath
Is golden gorse, or purple heath:
And now we hear in woodlands dim
Their unarticulated hymn,
Now walk through rippling waves of wheat,
Now sink in mats of clover sweet,
Or see before us from the lawn
The lark go up to greet the dawn!
All birds that love the English sky
Throng round my path when she is by:
The blackbird from a neighboring thorn
With music brims the cup of morn,
And in a thick, melodious rain
The mavis pours her mellow strain!
But only when my Katie's voice
Makes all the listening woods rejoice
I hear—with cheeks that flush and pale—
The passion of the nightingale!

Anon the pictures round her change,
And through an ancient town we range,
Whereto the shadowy memory clings
Of one of England's Saxon kings,
And which to shrine his fading fame
Still keeps his ashes and his name.

Quaint houses rise on either hand,
But still the airs are fresh and bland,
As if their gentle wings caressed
Some new-born village of the West.
A moment by the Norman tower
We pause; it is the Sabbath hour!
And o'er the city sinks and swells
The chime of old St. Mary's bells,
Which still resound in Katie's ears
As sweet as when in distant years
She heard them peal with jocund din
A merry English Christmas in!
We pass the abbey's ruined arch,
And statelier grows my Katie's march,
As round her, wearied with the taint
Of Transatlantic pine and paint,
She sees a thousand tokens cast
Of England's venerable Past!
Our reverent footsteps lastly claims
The younger chapel of St. James,
Which, though, as English records run,
Not old, had seen full many a sun,
Ere to the cold December gale
The thoughtful Pilgrim spread his sail.
There Katie in her childish days
Spelt out her prayers and lisped her praise,
And doubtless, as her beauty grew,
Did much as other maidens do—
Across the pews and down the aisle
Sent many a beau-bewildering smile,

And to subserve her spirit's need
Learned other things beside the creed!
There, too, to-day her knee she bows,
And by her one whose darker brows
Betray the Southern heart that burns
Beside her, and which only turns
Its thoughts to Heaven in one request,
Not all unworthy to be blest,
But rising from an earthlier pain
Than might beseem a Christian fane.
Ah! can the guileless maiden share
The wish that lifts that passionate prayer?
Is all at peace that breast within?
Good angels! warn her of the sin!
Alas! what boots it? who can save
A willing victim of the wave?
Who cleanse a soul that loves its guilt?
Or gather wine when wine is spilt?

We quit the holy house and gain
The open air; then, happy twain,
Adown familiar streets we go,
And now and then she turns to show,
With fears that all is changing fast,
Some spot that's sacred to her Past.
Here by this way, through shadows cool,
A little maid, she tripped to school;
And there each morning used to stop
Before a wonder of a shop

Where, built of apples and of pears,
Rose pyramids of golden spheres;
While, dangling in her dazzled sight,
Ripe cherries cast a crimson light,
And made her think of elfin lamps,
And feast and sport in fairy camps,
Whereat, upon her royal throne
(Most richly carved in cherry-stone),
Titania ruled, in queenly state,
The boisterous revels of the fête!
'Twas yonder, with their "horrid" noise,
Dismissed from books, she met the boys,
Who, with a barbarous scorn of girls,
Glanced slightly at her sunny curls,
And laughed and leaped as reckless by
As though no pretty face were nigh!
But—here the maiden grows demure—
Indeed she's not so *very* sure,
That in a year, or haply twain,
Who looked e'er failed to look again,
And sooth to say, I little doubt
(Some azure day, the truth will out!)
That certain baits in certain eyes
Caught many an unsuspecting prize;
And somewhere underneath these eaves
A budding flirt put forth its leaves!

Has not the sky a deeper blue,
Have not the trees a greener hue,

And bend they not with lordlier grace
And nobler shapes above the place
Where on one cloudless winter morn
My Katie to this life was born?
Ah, folly! long hath fled the hour
When love to sight gave keener power,
And lovers looked for special boons
In brighter flowers and larger moons.
But wave the foliage as it may,
And let the sky be ashen gray,
Thus much at least a manly youth
May hold—and yet not blush—as truth:
If near that blessed spot of earth
Which saw the cherished maiden's birth
No softer dews than usual rise,
And life there keeps its wonted guise,
Yet not the less that spot may seem
As lovely as a poet's dream;
And should a fervid faith incline
To make thereof a sainted shrine,
Who may deny that round us throng
A hundred earthly creeds as wrong,
But meaner far, which yet unblamed
Stalk by us and are not ashamed?
So, therefore, Katie, as our stroll
Ends at this portal, while you roll
Those lustrous eyes to catch each ray
That may recall some vanished day,
I—let them jeer and laugh who will—
Stoop down and kiss the sacred sill!

So strongly sometimes on the sense
These fancies hold their influence,
That in long well-known streets I stray
Like one who fears to lose his way.
The stranger, I, the native, she,
Myself, not Kate, had crossed the sea;
And changing place, and mixing times,
I walk in unfamiliar climes!
These houses, free to every breeze
That blows from warm Floridian seas,
Assume a massive English air,
And close around an English square;
While, if I issue from the town,
An English hill looks greenly down,
Or round me rolls an English park,
And in the Broad I hear the Larke!
Thus when, where woodland violets hide,
I rove with Katie at my side,
It scarce would seem amiss to say:
" Katie! my home lies far away,
  Beyond the pathless waste of brine,
  In a young land of palm and pine!
  There, by the tropic heats, the soul
  Is touched as if with living coal,
  And glows with such a fire as none
  Can feel beneath a Northern sun,
  Unless—my Katie's heart attest!—
  'Tis kindled in an English breast!
  Such is the land in which I live,
  And, Katie! such the soul I give.

Come! ere another morning beam,
We'll cleave the sea with wings of steam;
And soon, despite of storm or calm,
Beneath my native groves of palm,
Kind friends shall greet, with joy and pride,
The Southron and his English bride!"

————◆————

CAROLINA.

I.

The despot treads thy sacred sands,
Thy pines give shelter to his bands,
Thy sons stand by with idle hands,
            Carolina!
He breathes at ease thy airs of balm,
He scorns the lances of thy palm;
Oh! who shall break thy craven calm,
            Carolina!
Thy ancient fame is growing dim,
A spot is on thy garment's rim;
Give to the winds thy battle hymn,
            Carolina!

II.

Call on thy children of the hill,
Wake swamp and river, coast and rill,
Rouse all thy strength and all thy skill,
            Carolina!

Cite wealth and science, trade and art,
Touch with thy fire the cautious mart,
And pour thee through the people's heart,
                Carolina!
Till even the coward spurns his fears,
And all thy fields and fens and meres
Shall bristle like thy palm with spears,
                Carolina!

                III.

Hold up the glories of thy dead;
Say how thy elder children bled,
And point to Eutaw's battle-bed,
                Carolina!
Tell how the patriot's soul was tried,
And what his dauntless breast defied;
How Rutledge ruled and Laurens died,
                Carolina!
Cry! till thy summons, heard at last,
Shall fall like Marion's bugle-blast
Re-echoed from the haunted Past,
                Carolina!

                IV.

I hear a murmur as of waves
That grope their way through sunless caves,
Like bodies struggling in their graves,
                Carolina!
                4*

And now it deepens; slow and grand
It swells, as, rolling to the land,
An ocean broke upon thy strand,
   Carolina!
Shout! let it reach the startled Huns!
And roar with all thy festal guns!
It is the answer of thy sons,
   Carolina!

v.

They will not wait to hear thee call;
From Sachem's Head to Sumter's wall
Resounds the voice of hut and hall,
   Carolina!
No! thou hast not a stain, they say,
Or none save what the battle-day
Shall wash in seas of blood away,
   Carolina!
Thy skirts indeed the foe may part,
Thy robe be pierced with sword and dart,
They shall not touch thy noble heart,
   Carolina!

VI.

Ere thou shalt own the tyrant's thrall
Ten times ten thousand men must fall;
Thy corpse may hearken to his call,
   Carolina!

When, by thy bier, in mournful throngs
The women chant thy mortal wrongs,
'Twill be their own funereal songs,
    Carolina!
From thy dead breast by ruffians trod
No helpless child shall look to God;
All shall be safe beneath thy sod,
    Carolina!

VII.

Girt with such wills to do and bear,
Assured in right, and mailed in prayer,
Thou wilt not bow thee to despair,
    Carolina!
Throw thy bold banner to the breeze!
Front with thy ranks the threatening seas
Like thine own proud armorial trees,
    Carolina!
Fling down thy gauntlet to the Huns,
And roar the challenge from thy guns;
Then leave the future to thy sons,
    Carolina!

A CRY TO ARMS.

Ho! woodsmen of the mountain side!
 Ho! dwellers in the vales!
Ho! ye who by the chafing tide
 Have roughened in the gales!

Leave barn and byre, leave kin and cot,
  Lay by the bloodless spade;
Let desk, and case, and counter rot,
  And burn your books of trade.

The despot roves your fairest lands;
  And till he flies or fears,
Your fields must grow but armed bands,
  Your sheaves be sheaves of spears!
Give up to mildew and to rust
  The useless tools of gain;
And feed your country's sacred dust
  With floods of crimson rain!

Come, with the weapons at your call—
  With musket, pike, or knife;
He wields the deadliest blade of all
  Who lightest holds his life.
The arm that drives its unbought blows
  With all a patriot's scorn,
Might brain a tyrant with a rose,
  Or stab him with a thorn.

Does any falter? let him turn
  To some brave maiden's eyes,
And catch the holy fires that burn
  In those sublunar skies.
Oh! could you like your women feel.
  And in their spirit march,
A day might see your lines of steel
  Beneath the victor's arch.

What hope, O God! would not grow warm
  When thoughts like these give cheer?
The Lily calmly braves the storm,
  And shall the Palm-tree fear?
No! rather let its branches court
  The rack that sweeps the plain;
And from the Lily's regal port
  Learn how to breast the strain!

Ho! woodsmen of the mountain side!
  Ho! dwellers in the vales!
Ho! ye who by the roaring tide
  Have roughened in the gales!
Come! flocking gayly to the fight,
  From forest, hill, and lake;
We battle for our Country's right,
  And for the Lily's sake!

----·----

SERENADE.

Hide, happy damask, from the stars,
  What sleep enfolds behind your veil,
But open to the fairy cars
  On which the dreams of midnight sail;
And let the zephyrs rise and fall
  About her in the curtained gloom,
And then return to tell me all
  The silken secrets of the room.

Ah, dearest! may the elves that sway
　　Thy fancies come from emerald plots,
Where they have dozed and dreamed all day
　　In hearts of blue forget-me-nots.
And one perhaps shall whisper thus:
　　Awake! and light the darkness, Sweet!
While thou art revelling with us,
　　He watches in the lonely street.

WHY SILENT?

Why am I silent from year to year?
　　Needs must I sing on these blue March days?
What will you say, when I tell you here,
　　That already, I think, for a little praise,
　　　　I have paid too dear?

For, I know not why, when I tell my thought,
　　It seems as though I fling it away;
And the charm wherewith a fancy is fraught,
　　When secret, dies with the fleeting lay
　　　　Into which it is wrought.

So my butterfly-dreams their golden wings
　　But seldom unfurl from their chrysalis;
And thus I retain my loveliest things,
　　While the world, in its worldliness, does not miss
　　　　What a poet sings.

TWO PORTRAITS.

I.

You say, as one who shapes a life,
That you will never be a wife,

And, laughing lightly, ask my aid
To paint your future as a maid.

This is the portrait; and I take
The softest colors for your sake:

The springtime of your soul is dead,
And forty years have bent your head;

The lines are firmer round your mouth,
But still its smile is like the South.

Your eyes, grown deeper, are not sad,
Yet never more than gravely glad;

And the old charm still lurks within
The cloven dimple of your chin.

Some share, perhaps, of youthful gloss
Your cheek hath shed; but still across

The delicate ear are folded down
Those silken locks of chestnut brown;

Though here and there a thread of gray
Steals through them like a lunar ray.

One might suppose your life had passed
Unvexed by any troubling blast;

And such—for all that I foreknow—
May be the truth! The deeper woe!

A loveless heart is seldom stirred;
And sorrow shuns the mateless bird;

But ah! through cares alone we reach
The happiness which mocketh speech;

In the white courts beyond the stars
The noblest brow is seamed with scars;

And they on earth who've wept the most
Sit highest of the heavenly host.

Grant that your maiden life hath sped
In music o'er a golden bed,

With rocks, and winds, and storms at truce,
And not without a noble use;

Yet are you happy? In your air
I see a nameless want appear,

And a faint shadow on your cheek
Tells what the lips refuse to speak.

You have had all a maid could hope
In the most cloudless horoscope:

The strength that cometh from above;
A Christian mother's holy love;

And always at your soul's demand
A brother's, sister's heart and hand.

Small need your heart hath had to roam
Beyond the circle of your home ;

And yet upon your wish attends
A loving throng of genial friends.

What, in a lot so sweet as this,
Is wanting to complete your bliss ?

And to what secret shall I trace
The clouds that sometimes cross your face,

And that sad look which now and then
Comes, disappears, and comes again,

And dies reluctantly away
In those clear eyes of azure gray?

At best, and after all, the place
You fill with such a serious grace,

Hath much to try a woman's heart,
And you but play a painful part.

The world around, with little ruth,
Still laughs at maids who have not youth,

And, right or wrong, the old maid rests
The victim of its paltry jests,

And still is doomed to meet and bear
Its pitying smile or furtive sneer.

These are indeed but petty things,
And yet they touch some hearts like stings.

But I acquit you of the shame
Of being unresisting game ;

For you are of such tempered clay
As turns far stronger shafts away,

And all that foes or fools could guide
Would only curl that lip of pride.

How then, O weary one! explain
The sources of that hidden pain ?

Alas! you have divined at length
How little you have used your strength,

Which, with who knows what human good,
Lies buried in that maidenhood,

Where, as amid a field of flowers,
You have but played with April showers.

Ah ! we would wish the world less fair,
If Spring alone adorned the year,

And Autumn came not with its fruit,
And Autumn hymns were ever mute.

So I remark without surprise
That, as the unvarying season flies,

From day to night, and night to day,
You sicken of your endless May.

In this poor life we may not cross
One virtuous instinct without loss,

And the soul grows not to its height
Till love calls forth its utmost might.

Not blind to all you might have been,
And with some consciousness of sin—

Because with love you sometimes played,
And choice, not fate, hath kept you maid—

You feel that you must pass from earth
But half-acquainted with its worth,

And that within your heart are deeps
In which a nobler woman sleeps;

That not the maiden, but the wife
Grasps the whole lesson of a life,

While such as you but sit and dream
Along the surface of its stream.

And doubtless sometimes, all unsought,
There comes upon your hour of thought,

Despite the struggles of your will,
A sense of something absent still;

And then you cannot help but yearn
To love and be beloved in turn,

As they are loved, and love, who live
As love were all that life could give;

And in a transient clasp or kiss
Crowd an eternity of bliss;

They who of every mortal joy
Taste always twice, nor feel them cloy,

Or, if woes come, in Sorrow's hour
Are strengthened by a double power.

II.

Here ends my feeble sketch of what
Might, but will never be your lot;

And I foresee how oft these rhymes
Shall make you smile in after-times.

If I have read your nature right,
It only waits a spark of light;

And when that comes, as come it must,
It will not fall on arid dust,

Nor yet on that which breaks to flame
In the first blush of maiden shame;

But on a heart which, even at rest,
Is warmer than an April nest,

Where, settling soft, that spark shall creep
About as gently as a sleep;

Still stealing on with pace so slow
Yourself will scarcely feel the glow,

Till after many and many a day,
Although no gleam its course betray,

It shall attain the inmost shrine,
And wrap it in a fire divine!

I know not when or whence indeed
Shall fall and burst the burning seed,

But oh! once kindled, it will blaze,
I know, for ever! By its rays

You will perceive, with subtler eyes,
The meaning in the earth and skies,

Which, with their animated chain
Of grass and flowers, and sun and rain,

Of green below, and blue above,
Are but a type of married love.

You will perceive that in the breast
The germs of many virtues rest,

Which, ere they feel a lover's breath,
Lie in a temporary death;

And till the heart is wooed and won
It is an earth without a sun.

III.

But now, stand forth as sweet as life!
And let me paint you as a wife.

I note some changes in your face,
And in your mien a graver grace;

Yet the calm forehead lightly bears
Its weight of twice a score of years;

And that one love which on this earth
Can wake the heart to all its worth,

And to their height can lift and bind
The powers of soul, and sense, and mind,

Hath not allowed a charm to fade —
And the wife's lovelier than the maid.

An air of still, though bright repose
Tells that a tender hand bestows

All that a generous manhood may
To make your life one bridal day,

While the kind eyes betray no less,
In their blue depths of tenderness,

That you have learned the truths which lie
Behind that holy mystery,

Which, with its blisses and its woes,
Nor man nor maiden ever knows.

If now, as to the eyes of one
Whose glance not even thought can shun,

Your soul lay open to my view,
I, looking all its nature through,

Could see no incompleted part,
For the whole woman warms your heart.

I connot tell how many dead
You number in the cycles fled,

And you but look the more serene
For all the griefs you may have seen,

As you had gathered from the dust
The flowers of Peace, and Hope, and Trust.

Your smile is even sweeter now
That when it lit your maiden brow,

And that which wakes this gentler charm
Coos at this moment on your arm.

Your voice was always soft in youth,
And had the very sound of truth,

But never were its tones so mild
Until you blessed your earliest child;

And when to soothe some little wrong
It melts into a mother's song,

The same strange sweetness which in years
Long vanished filled the eyes with tears,

And (even when mirthful) gave always
A pathos to your girlish lays,

Falls, with perchance a deeper thrill,
Upon the breathless listener still.

I cannot guess in what fair spot
The chance of Time hath fixed your lot,

Nor can I name what manly breast
Gives to that head a welcome rest;

I cannot tell if partial Fate
Hath made you poor, or rich, or great;

But oh! whatever be your place,
I never saw a form or face

To which more plainly hath been lent
The blessing of a full content!

———•———

CHARLESTON.

Calm as that second summer which precedes
   The first fall of the snow,
In the broad sunlight of heroic deeds,
   The City bides the foe.

As yet, behind their ramparts stern and proud,
   Her bolted thunders sleep—
Dark Sumter, like a battlemented cloud,
   Looms o'er the solemn deep.

No Calpe frowns from lofty cliff or scar
   To guard the holy strand;
But Moultrie holds in leash her dogs of war
   Above the level sand.

And down the dunes a thousand guns lie couched,
   Unseen, beside the flood—
Like tigers in some Orient jungle crouched
   That wait and watch for blood.

Meanwhile, through streets still echoing with trade,
   Walk grave and thoughtful men,

Whose hands may one day wield the patriot's blade
    As lightly as the pen.

And maidens, with such eyes as would grow dim
    Over a bleeding hound,
Seem each one to have caught the strength of him
    Whose sword she sadly bound.

Thus girt without and garrisoned at home,
    Day patient following day,
Old Charleston looks from roof, and spire, and dome,
    Across her tranquil bay.

Ships, through a hundred foes, from Saxon lands
    And spicy Indian ports,
Bring Saxon steel and iron to her hands,
    And Summer to her courts.

But still, along yon dim Atlantic line,
    The only hostile smoke
Creeps like a harmless mist above the brine,
    From some frail, floating oak.

Shall the Spring dawn, and she still clad in smiles,
    And with an unscathed brow,
Rest in the strong arms of her palm-crowned isles,
    As fair and free as now?

We know not; in the temple of the Fates
    God has inscribed her doom;
And, all untroubled in her faith, she waits
    The triumph or the tomb.

RIPLEY.

Rich in red honors, that upon him lie
  As lightly as the Summer dews
Fall where he won his fame beneath the sky
  Of tropic Vera Cruz;

Bold scorner of the cant that has its birth
  In feeble or in failing powers;
A lover of all frank and genial mirth
  That wreathes the sword with flowers;

He moves amid the warriors of the day,
  Just such a soldier as the art
That builds its trophies upon human clay
  Moulds of a cheerful heart.

I see him in the battle that shall shake,
  Ere long, old Sumter's haughty crown,
And from their dreams of peaceful traffic wake
  The wharves of yonder town;

As calm as one would greet a pleasant guest,
  And quaff a cup to love and life,
He hurls his deadliest thunders with a jest,
  And laughs amid the strife.

Yet not the gravest soldier of them all
  Surveys a field with broader scope;
And who behind that sea-encircled wall
  Fights with a loftier hope?

Gay Chieftain! on the crimson rolls of Fame
　　Thy deeds are written with the sword;
But there are gentler thoughts which, with thy name,
　　Thy country's page shall hoard.

A nature of that rare and happy cast
　　Which looks, unsteeled, on murder's face;
Through what dark scenes of bloodshed hast thou
　　　　passed,
　　Yet lost no social grace?

So, when the bard depicts thee, thou shalt wield
　　The weapon of a tyrant's doom,
Round which, inscribed with many a well-fought field,
　　The rose of joy shall bloom.

ETHNOGENESIS.

*Written during the meeting of the first Southern Congress, at Montgomery,
February, 1861.*

I.

Hath not the morning dawned with added light?
And shall not evening call another star
Out of the infinite regions of the night,
To mark this day in Heaven?　At last, we are
A nation among nations; and the world
Shall soon behold in many a distant port
　　　　Another flag unfurled!
Now, come what may, whose favor need we court?

And, under God, whose thunder need we fear?
    Thank Him who placed us here
Beneath so kind a sky—the very sun
Takes part with us; and on our errands run
All breezes of the ocean; dew and rain
Do noiseless battle for us; and the Year,
And all the gentle daughters in her train,
March in our ranks, and in our service wield
    Long spears of golden grain!
A yellow blossom as her fairy shield,
June flings her azure banner to the wind,
    While in the order of their birth
Her sisters pass, and many an ample field
Grows white beneath their steps, till now, behold,
    Its endless sheets unfold
THE SNOW OF SOUTHERN SUMMERS! Let the earth
Rejoice! beneath those fleeces soft and warm
    Our happy land shall sleep
    In a repose as deep
  As if we lay intrenched behind
Whole leagues of Russian ice and Arctic storm!

II.

And what if, mad with wrongs themselves have
    wrought,
    In their own treachery caught,
    By their own fears made bold,
    And leagued with him of old,
Who long since in the limits of the North

Set up his evil throne, and warred with God—
What if, both mad and blinded in their rage,
Our foes should fling us down their mortal gage,
And with a hostile step profane our sod!
We shall not shrink, my brothers, but go forth
To meet them, marshalled by the Lord of Hosts,
And overshadowed by the mighty ghosts
Of Moultrie and of Eutaw—who shall foil
Auxiliars such as these?   Nor these alone,
   But every stock and stone
   Shall help us; but the very soil,
And all the generous wealth it gives to toil,
And all for which we love our noble land,
Shall fight beside, and through us; sea and strand,
   The heart of woman, and her hand,
Tree, fruit, and flower, and every influence,
   Gentle, or grave, or grand;
   The winds in our defence
Shall seem to blow; to us the hills shall lend
   Their firmness and their calm;
And in our stiffened sinews we shall blend
   The strength of pine and palm!

III.

Nor would we shun the battle-ground.
   Though weak as we are strong;
Call up the clashing elements around,
   And test the right and wrong!
On one side, creeds that dare to teach
What Christ and Paul refrained to preach;

Codes built upon a broken pledge,
And Charity that whets a poniard's edge;
Fair schemes that leave the neighboring poor
To starve and shiver at the schemer's door,
While in the world's most liberal ranks enrolled,
He turns some vast philanthropy to gold;
Religion, taking every mortal form
But that a pure and Christian faith makes warm,
Where not to vile fanatic passion urged,
Or not in vague philosophies submerged,
Repulsive with all Pharisaic leaven,
And making laws to stay the laws of Heaven!
And on the other, scorn of sordid gain,
Unblemished honor, truth without a stain,
Faith, justice, reverence, charitable wealth,
And, for the poor and humble, laws which give,
Not the mean right to buy the right to live,
  But life, and home, and health!
To doubt the end were want of trust in God,
  Who, if he has decreed
 That we must pass a redder sea
Than that which rang to Miriam's holy glee,
  Will surely raise at need
  A Moses with his rod!

IV.

But let our fears—if fears we have—be still,
And turn us to the future! Could we climb
Some mighty Alp, and view the coming time,

The rapturous sight would fill
Our eyes with happy tears!
Not only for the glories which the years
Shall bring us; not for lands from sea to sea,
And wealth, and power, and peace, though these shall
be;
But for the distant peoples we shall bless,
And the hushed murmurs of a world's distress:
For, to give labor to the poor,
The whole sad planet o'er,
And save from want and crime the humblest door,
Is one among the many ends for which
God makes us great and rich!
The hour perchance is not yet wholly ripe
When all shall own it, but the type
Whereby we shall be known in every land
Is that vast gulf which lips our Southern strand,
And through the cold, untempered ocean pours
Its genial streams, that far off Arctic shores
May sometimes catch upon the softened breeze
Strange tropic warmth and hints of summer seas.

CHRISTMAS.

How grace this hallowed day?
Shall happy bells, from yonder ancient spire,
Send their glad greetings to each Christmas fire
Round which the children play?

Alas! for many a moon,
That tongueless tower hath cleaved the Sabbath air,
Mute as an obelisk of ice, aglare
    Beneath an Arctic noon.

Shame to the foes that drown
Our psalms of worship with their impious drum,
The sweetest chimes in all the land lie dumb
    In some far rustic town.

There, let us think, they keep,
Of the dead Yules which here beside the sea
They've ushered in with old-world, English glee,
    Some echoes in their sleep.

How shall we grace the day?
With feast, and song, and dance, and antique sports,
And shout of happy children in the courts,
    And tales of ghost and fay?

Is there indeed a door,
Where the old pastimes, with their lawful noise,
And all the merry round of Christmas joys,
    Could enter as of yore?

Would not some pallid face
Look in upon the banquet, calling up
Dread shapes of battles in the wassail cup,
    And trouble all the place?

How could we bear the mirth,
While some loved reveller of a year ago
    5*

Keeps his mute Christmas now beneath the snow,
    In cold Virginian earth ?

        How shall we grace the day ?
Ah ! let the thought that on this holy morn
The Prince of Peace—the Prince of Peace was born,
    Employ us, while we pray !

        Pray for the peace which long
Hath left this tortured land, and haply now
Holds its white court on some far mountain's brow,
    There hardly safe from wrong !

        Let every sacred fane
Call its sad votaries to the shrine of God,
And, with the cloister and the tented sod,
    Join in one solemn strain !

        With pomp of Roman form,
With the grave ritual brought from England's shore,
And with the simple faith which asks no more
    Than that the heart be warm !

        He, who, till time shall cease,
Will watch that earth, where once, not all in vain,
He died to give us peace, may not disdain
    A prayer whose theme is—peace.

        Perhaps ere yet the Spring
Hath died into the Summer, over all
The land, the peace of His vast love shall fall,
    Like some protecting wing.

Oh, ponder what it means!
Oh, turn the rapturous thought in every way!
Oh, give the vision and the fancy play,
        And shape the coming scenes!

        Peace in the quiet dales,
Made rankly fertile by the blood of men,
Peace in the woodland, and the lonely glen,
        Peace in the peopled vales!

        Peace in the crowded town,
Peace in a thousand fields of waving grain,
Peace in the highway and the flowery lane,
        Peace on the wind-swept down!

        Peace on the farthest seas,
Peace in our sheltered bays and ample streams,
Peace wheresoe'er our starry garland gleams,
        And peace in every breeze!

        Peace on the whirring marts,
Peace where the scholar thinks, the hunter roams,
Peace, God of Peace! peace, peace, in all our homes,
        And peace in all our hearts!

LA BELLE JUIVE.

Is it because your sable hair
Is folded over brows that wear
At times a too imperial air;

Or is it that the thoughts which rise
In those dark orbs do seek disguise
Beneath the lids of Eastern eyes ;

That choose whatever pose or place
May chance to please, in you I trace
The noblest woman of your race ?

The crowd is sauntering at its ease,
And humming like a hive of bees—
You take your seat and touch the keys :

I do not hear the giddy throng ;
The sea avenges Israel's wrong,
And on the wind floats Miriam's song !

You join me with a stately grace ;
Music to Poesy gives place ;
Some grand emotion lights your face :

At once I stand by Mizpeh's walls ;
With smiles the martyred daughter falls,
And desolate are Mizpeh's halls !

Intrusive babblers come between ;
With calm, pale brow and lofty mien,
You thread the circle like a queen !

Then sweeps the royal Esther by ;
The deep devotion in her eye
Is looking " If I die, I die ! "

You stroll the garden's flowery walks;
The plants to me are grainless stalks,
And Ruth to old Naomi talks.

Adopted child of Judah's creed,
Like Judah's daughters, true at need,
I see you mid the alien seed.

I watch afar the gleaner sweet;
I wake like Boaz in the wheat,
And find you lying at my feet!

My feet! Oh! if the spell that lures
My heart through all these dreams endures,
How soon shall I be stretched at yours!

AN EXOTIC.

Not in a climate near the sun
  Did the cloud with its trailing fringes float,
Whence, white as the down of an angel's plume,
  Fell the snows of her brow and throat.

And the ground had been rich for a thousand years
  With the blood of heroes, and sages, and kings,
Where the rose that blooms in her exquisite cheek
  Unfolded the flush of its wings.

On a land where the faces are fair, though pale
  As a moonlit mist when the winds are still,

She breaks like a morning in Paradise
  Through the palms of an orient hill.

Her beauty, perhaps, were all too bright,
  But about her there broods some delicate spell,
Whence the wondrous charm of the girl grows soft
  As the light in an English dell.

There is not a story of faith and truth
  On the starry scroll of her country's fame,
But has helped to shape her stately mien,
  And to touch her soul with flame.

I sometimes forget, as she sweeps me a bow,
  That I gaze on a simple English maid,
And I bend my head, as if to a queen
  Who is courting my lance and blade.

Once, as we read, in a curtained niche,
  A poet who sang of her sea-throned isle,
There was something of Albion's mighty Bess
  In the flash of her haughty smile.

She seemed to gather from every age
  All the greatness of England about her there,
And my fancy wove a royal crown
  Of the dusky gold of her hair.

But it was no queen to whom that day,
  In the dim green shade of a trellised vine,
I whispered a hope that had somewhat to do
  With a small white hand in mine.

The Tudor had vanished, and, as I spoke,
    'Twas herself looked out of her frank brown eye,
And an answer was burning upon her face,
    Ere I caught the low reply.

What was it! Nothing the world need know—
    The stars saw our parting! Enough, that then
I walked from the porch with the tread of a king,
    And she was a queen again!

THE ROSEBUDS.

Yes, in that dainty ivory shrine,
With those three pallid buds, I twine
And fold away a dream divine!

One night they lay upon a breast
Where Love hath made his fragrant nest,
And throned me as a life-long guest.

Near that chaste heart they seemed to me
Types of far fairer flowers to be—
The rosebuds of a human tree!

Buds that shall bloom beside my hearth,
And there be held of richer worth
Than all the kingliest gems of earth.

Ah me! the pathos of the thought!
I had not deemed she wanted aught;
Yet what a tenderer charm it wrought!

I know not if she marked the flame
That lit my cheek, but not from shame,
When one sweet image dimly came.

There was a murmur soft and low;
White folds of cambric, parted slow;
And little fingers played with snow!

How far my fancy dared to stray,
A lover's reverence needs not say—
Enough—the vision passed away!

Passed in a mist of happy tears,
While something in my tranced ears
Hummed like the future in a seer's!

———

A MOTHER'S WAIL.

My babe! my tiny babe! my only babe!
My single rose-bud in a crown of thorns!
My lamp that in that narrow hut of life,
Whence I looked forth upon a night of storm!
Burned with the lustre of the moon and stars!

My babe! my tiny babe! my only babe!
Behold the bud is gone! the thorns remain!
My lamp hath fallen from its niche—ah, me!
Earth drinks the fragrant flame, and I am left
Forever and forever in the dark!

My babe! my babe! my own and only babe!
Where art thou now?   If somewhere in the sky
An angel hold thee in his radiant arms,
I challenge him to clasp thy tender form
With half the fervor of a mother's love!

Forgive me, Lord! forgive my reckless grief!
Forgive me that this rebel, selfish heart
Would almost make me jealous for my child,
Though thy own lap enthroned him.   Lord, thou hast
So many such!   I have—ah! had but one!

O yet once more, my babe, to hear thy cry!
O yet once more, my babe, to see thy smile!
O yet once more to feel against my breast
Those cool, soft hands, that warm, wet, eager mouth,
With the sweet sharpness of its budding pearls!

But it must never, never more be mine
To mark the growing meaning in thine eyes,
To watch thy soul unfolding leaf by leaf,
Or catch, with ever fresh surprise and joy,
Thy dawning recognitions of the world.

Three different shadows of thyself, my babe,
Change with each other while I weep.   The first,

The sweetest, yet the not least fraught with pain,
Clings like my living boy around my neck,
Or purrs and murmurs softly at my feet!

Another is a little mound of earth;
That comes the oftenest, darling! In my dreams,
I see it beaten by the midnight rain,
Or chilled beneath the moon.   Ah! what a couch
For that which I have shielded from a breath
That would not stir the violets on thy grave!

The third, my precious babe! the third, O Lord!
Is a fair cherub face beyond the stars,
Wearing the roses of a mystic bliss,
Yet sometimes not unsaddened by a glance
Turned earthward on a mother in her woe!

This is the vision, Lord, that I would keep
Before me always.   But, alas! as yet,
It is the dimmest and the rarest, too!
O touch my sight, or break the cloudy bars
That hide it, lest I madden where I kneel!

OUR WILLIE.

'Twas merry Christmas when he came,
Our little boy beneath the sod;
And brighter burned the Christmas flame,
And merrier sped the Christmas game,

Because within the house there lay
A shape as tiny as a fay—
  The Christmas gift of God!
In wreaths and garlands on the walls
The holly hung its ruby balls,
  The mistletoe its pearls;
And a Christmas tree's fantastic fruits
Woke laughter like a choir of flutes
  From happy boys and girls.
For the mirth, which else had swelled as shrill
As a school let loose to its errant will,
  Was softened by the thought,
That in a dim hushed room above
A mother's pains in a mother's love
  Were only just forgot.
The jest, the tale, the toast, the glee,
  All took a sober tone;
We spoke of the babe upstairs, as we
Held festival for him alone.
When the bells rang in the Christmas morn,
It scarcely seemed a sin to say
That they rang because that babe was born,
Not less than for the sacred day.
Ah! Christ forgive us for the crime
Which drowned the memories of the time
  In a merely mortal bliss!
We owned the error when the mirth
Of another Christmas lit the hearth
  Of every home but this.
When, in that lonely burial-ground,

With every Christmas sight and sound
Removed or shunned, we kept
A mournful Christmas by the mound
Where little Willie slept!

Ah, hapless mother! darling wife!
I might say nothing more,
And the dull cold world would hold
The story of that precious life
      As amply told!
Shall we, shall you and I, before
That world's unsympathetic eyes
Lay other relics from our store
      Of tender memories?
What could it know of the joy and love
That throbbed and smiled and wept above
      An unresponsive thing?
And who could share the ecstatic thrill
With which we watched the upturned bill
Of our bird at its living spring?
Shall we tell how in the time gone by,
Beneath all changes of the sky,
And in an ordinary home
      Amid the city's din,
Life was to us a crystal dome,
      Our babe the flame therein?
Ah! this were jargon on the mart;
And though some gentle friend,
And many and many a suffering heart,
Would weep and comprehend,

Yet even these might fail to see
What we saw daily in the child—
Not the mere creature undefiled,
But the winged cherub soon to be.
That wandering hand which seemed to reach
  At angel finger-tips,
And that murmur like a mystic speech
  Upon the rosy lips,
That something in the serious face
Holier than even its infant grace,
And that rapt gaze on empty space,
Which made us, half believing, say,
" Ah, little wide-eyed seer! who knows
But that for you this chamber glows
With stately shapes and solemn shows ?"
Which touched us, too, with vague alarms,
Lest in the circle of our arms
We held a being less akin
To his parents in a world of sin
Than to beings not of clay:
How could we speak in human phrase,
Of such scarce earthly traits and ways,
  What would not seem
  A doting dream,
In the creed of these sordid days?
  No! let us keep
  Deep, deep,
In sorrowing heart and aching brain,
This story hidden with the pain.

Which, since that blue October night
When Willie vanished from our sight,
Must haunt us even in our sleep.
In the gloom of the chamber where he died,
And by that grave which, through our care,
From Yule to Yule of every year,
Is made like Spring to bloom;
And where, at times, we catch the sigh
As of an angel floating nigh,
Who longs but has not power to tell
That in that violet-shrouded cell
Lies nothing better than the shell
Which he had cast aside—
By that sweet grave, in that dark room,
We may weave at will for each other's ear,
Of that life, and that love, and that early doom,
The tale which is shadowed here:
To us alone it will always be
As fresh as our own misery;
But enough, alas! for the world is said,
In the brief " Here lieth " of the dead!

———

CARMEN TRIUMPHALE.

Go forth and bid the land rejoice,
 Yet not too gladly, O my song!
 Breathe softly, as if mirth would wrong
The solemn rapture of thy voice.

Be nothing lightly done or said
  This happy day!   Our joy should flow
  Accordant with the lofty woe
That wails above the noble dead.

Let him whose brow and breast were calm
  While yet the battle lay with God,
  Look down upon the crimson sod
And gravely wear his mournful palm;

And him, whose heart still weak from fear
  Beats all too gayly for the time,
  Know that intemperate glee is crime
While one dead hero claims a tear.

Yet go thou forth, my song! and thrill,
  With sober joy, the troubled days;
  A nation's hymn of grateful praise
May not be hushed for private ill.

Our foes are fallen!   Flash, ye wires!
  The mighty tidings far and nigh!
  Ye cities! write them on the sky
In purple and in emerald fires!

They came with many a haughty boast;
  Their threats were heard on every breeze;
  They darkened half the neighboring seas;
And swooped like vultures on the coast.

False recreants in all knightly strife,
  Their way was wet with woman's tears;

Behind them flamed the toil of years,
And bloodshed stained the sheaves of life.

They fought as tyrants fight, or slaves;
    God gave the dastards to our hands;
    Their bones are bleaching on the sands,
Or mouldering slow in shallow graves.

What though we hear about our path
    The heavens with howls of vengeance rent?
    The venom of their hate is spent;
We need not heed their fangless wrath.

Meantime the stream they strove to chain
    Now drinks a thousand springs, and sweeps
    With broadening breast, and mightier deeps,
And rushes onward to the main;

While down the swelling current glides
    Our Ship of State before the blast,
    With streamers poured from every mast,
Her thunders roaring from her sides.

Lord! bid the frenzied tempest cease,
    Hang out thy rainbow on the sea!
    Laugh round her, waves! in silver glee,
And speed her to the port of peace!

ADDRESS DELIVERED AT THE OPENING
OF THE NEW THEATRE AT RICHMOND.

A PRIZE POEM.

A fairy ring
Drawn in the crimson of a battle-plain—
From whose weird circle every loathsome thing
    And sight and sound of pain
Are banished, while about it in the air,
And from the ground, and from the low-hung skies,
    Throng, in a vision fair
As ever lit a prophet's dying eyes,
    Gleams of that unseen world
That lies about us, rainbow-tinted shapes
    With starry wings unfurled,
Poised for a moment on such airy capes
    As pierce the golden foam
    Of sunset's silent main—
Would image what in this enchanted dome,
    Amid the night of war and death
In which the armed city draws its breath,
    We have built up!
For though no wizard wand or magic cup
    The spell hath wrought,
Within this charmed fane, we ope the gates
    Of that divinest Fairy-land,
    Where under loftier fates
Than rule the vulgar earth on which we stand,
Move the bright creatures of the realm of thought.

6

Shut for one happy evening from the flood
That roars around us, here you may behold—
    As if a desert way
    Could blossom and unfold
    A garden fresh with May—
Substantialized in breathing flesh and blood,
    Souls that upon the poet's page
    Have lived from age to age,
And yet have never donned this mortal clay.
    A golden strand
Shall sometimes spread before you like the isle
    Where fair Miranda's smile
Met the sweet stranger whom the father's art
    Had led unto her heart,
Which, like a bud that waited for the light,
    Burst into bloom at sight!
Love shall grow softer in each maiden's eyes
As Juliet leans her cheek upon her hand,
    And prattles to the night.
    Anon, a reverend form,
    With tattered robe and forehead bare,
That challenge all the torments of the air,
        Goes by!
And the pent feelings choke in one long sigh,
While, as the mimic thunder rolls, you hear
    The noble wreck of Lear
Reproach like things of life the ancient skies,
    And commune with the storm!
Lo! next a dim and silent chamber where,
Wrapt in glad dreams in which, perchance, the Moor
    Tells his strange story o'er,

The gentle Desdemona chastely lies,
Unconscious of the loving murderer nigh.
    Then through a hush like death
    Stalks Denmark's mailèd ghost!
And Hamlet enters with that thoughtful breath
Which is the trumpet to a countless host
Of reasons, but which wakes no deed from sleep;
    For while it calls to strife,
He pauses on the very brink of fact
To toy as with the shadow of an act,
And utter those wise saws that cut so deep
    Into the core of life!

    Nor shall be wanting many a scene
    Where forms of more familiar mien,
Moving through lowlier pathways, shall present
    The world of every day,
Such as it whirls along the busy quay,
Or sits beneath a rustic orchard wall,
Or floats about a fashion-freighted hall,
Or toils in attics dark the night away.
Love, hate, grief, joy, gain, glory, shame, shall meet,
As in the round wherein our lives are pent;
    Chance for a while shall seem to reign,
While Goodness roves like Guilt about the street,
    And Guilt looks innocent.
But all at last shall vindicate the right,
Crime shall be meted with its proper pain,
Motes shall be taken from the doubter's sight,
And Fortune's general justice rendered plain.

Of honest laughter there shall be no dearth,
Wit shall shake hands with humor grave and sweet,
Our wisdom shall not be too wise for mirth,
Nor kindred follies want a fool to greet.
As sometimes from the meanest spot of earth
A sudden beauty unexpected starts,
So you shall find some germs of hidden worth
    Within the vilest hearts;
And now and then, when in those moods that
    turn
To the cold Muse that whips a fault with sneers,
You shall, perchance, be strangely touched to learn
    You've struck a spring of tears!

But while we lead you thus from change to change,
Shall we not find within our ample range
Some type to elevate a people's heart—
Some hero who shall teach a hero's part
    In this distracted time?
Rise from thy sleep of ages, noble Tell!
And, with the Alpine thunders of thy voice,
As if across the billows unenthralled
Thy Alps unto the Alleghanies called,
    Bid Liberty rejoice!
Proclaim upon this trans-Atlantic strand
The deeds which, more than their own awful mien
Make every crag of Switzerland sublime!
And say to those whose feeble souls would lean,
Not on themselves, but on some outstretched hand,
That once a single mind sufficed to quell

The malice of a tyrant; let them know
That each may crowd in every well-aimed blow,
Not the poor strength alone of arm and brand,
But the whole spirit of a mighty land!

Bid Liberty rejoice!   Aye, though its day
Be far or near, these clouds shall yet be red
With the large promise of the coming ray.
Meanwhile, with that calm courage which can smile
Amid the terrors of the wildest fray,
Let us among the charms of Art awhile
    Fleet the deep gloom away;
Nor yet forget that on each hand and head
Rest the dear rights for which we fight and pray.

———•———

THE COTTON BOLL.

While I recline
At ease beneath
This immemorial pine,
Small sphere!
(By dusky fingers brought this morning here
And shown with boastful smiles),
I turn thy cloven sheath,
Through which the soft white fibres peer,
That, with their gossamer bands,
Unite, like love, the sea-divided lands,
And slowly, thread by thread,
Draw forth the folded strands,

Than which the trembling line,
By whose frail help yon startled spider fled
Down the tall spear-grass from his swinging bed,
Is scarce more fine;
And as the tangled skein
Unravels in my hands,
Betwixt me and the noonday light,
A veil seems lifted, and for miles and miles
The landscape broadens on my sight,
As, in the little boll, there lurked a spell
Like that which, in the ocean shell,
With mystic sound,
Breaks down the narrow walls that hem us round,
And turns some city lane
Into the restless main,
With all his capes and isles!

Yonder bird,
Which floats, as if at rest,
In those blue tracts above the thunder, where
No vapors cloud the stainless air,
And never sound is heard,
Unless at such rare time
When, from the City of the Blest,
Rings down some golden chime,
Sees not from his high place
So vast a cirque of summer space
As widens round me in one mighty field,
Which, rimmed by seas and sands,
Doth hail its earliest daylight in the beams

Of gray Atlantic dawns ;
And, broad as realms made up of many lands,
Is lost afar
Behind the crimson hills and purple lawns
Of sunset, among plains which roll their streams
Against the Evening Star !
And lo !
To the remotest point of sight,
Although I gaze upon no waste of snow,
The endless field is white ;
And the whole landscape glows,
For many a shining league away,
With such accumulated light
As Polar lands would flash beneath a tropic day !
Nor lack there (for the vision grows,
And the small charm within my hands—
More potent even than the fabled one,
Which oped whatever golden mystery
Lay hid in fairy wood or magic vale,
The curious ointment of the Arabian tale—
Beyond all mortal sense
Doth stretch my sight's horizon, and I see,
Beneath its simple influence,
As if with Uriel's crown,
I stood in some great temple of the Sun,
And looked, as Uriel, down!)
Nor lack there pastures rich and fields all green
With all the common gifts of God,
For temperate airs and torrid sheen
Weave Edens of the sod ;

Through lands which look one sea of billowy gold
Broad rivers wind their devious ways;
A hundred isles in their embraces fold
A hundred luminous bays;
And through yon purple haze
Vast mountains lift their plumed peaks cloud-
    crowned;
And, save where up their sides the ploughman creeps,
An unhewn forest girds them grandly round,
In whose dark shades a future navy sleeps!
Ye Stars, which, though unseen, yet with me gaze
Upon this loveliest fragment of the earth!
Thou Sun, that kindlest all thy gentlest rays
Above it, as to light a favorite hearth!
Ye Clouds, that in your temples in the West
See nothing brighter than its humblest flowers!
And you, ye Winds, that on the ocean's breast
Are kissed to coolness ere ye reach its bowers!
Bear witness with me in my song of praise,
And tell the world that, since the world began,
No fairer land hath fired a poet's lays,
Or given a home to man!

But these are charms already widely blown!
His be the meed whose pencil's trace
Hath touched our very swamps with grace,
And round whose tuneful way
All Southern laurels bloom;
The Poet of "The Woodlands," unto whom
Alike are known

The flute's low breathing and the trumpet's tone,
And the soft west wind's sighs;
But who shall utter all the debt,
O Land wherein all powers are met
That bind a people's heart,
The world doth owe thee at this day,
And which it never can repay,
Yet scarcely deigns to own!
Where sleeps the poet who shall fitly sing
The source wherefrom doth spring
That mighty commerce which, confined
To the mean channels of no selfish mart,
Goes out to every shore
Of this broad earth, and throngs the sea with ships
That bear no thunders; hushes hungry lips
In alien lands;
Joins with a delicate web remotest strands;
And gladdening rich and poor,
Doth gild Parisian domes,
Or feed the cottage-smoke of English homes,
And only bounds its blessings by mankind!
In offices like these, thy mission lies,
My Country! and it shall not end
As long as rain shall fall and Heaven bend
In blue above thee; though thy foes be hard
And cruel as their weapons, it shall guard
Thy hearth-stones as a bulwark; make thee great
In white and bloodless state;
And haply, as the years increase—

Still working through its humbler reach
With that large wisdom which the ages teach—
Revive the half-dead dream of universal peace !
As men who labor in that mine
Of Cornwall, hollowed out beneath the bed
Of ocean, when a storm rolls overhead,
Hear the dull booming of the world of brine
Above them, and a mighty muffled roar
Of winds and waters, yet toil calmly on,
And split the rock, and pile the massive ore,
Or carve a niche, or shape the archëd roof;
So I, as calmly, weave my woof
Of song, chanting the days to come,
Unsilenced, though the quiet summer air
Stirs with the bruit of battles, and each dawn
Wakes from its starry silence to the hum
Of many gathering armies.   Still,
In that we sometimes hear,
Upon the Northern winds, the voice of woe
Not wholly drowned in triumph, though I know
The end must crown us, and a few brief years
Dry all our tears,
I may not sing too gladly.   To Thy will
Resigned, O Lord ! we cannot all forget
That there is much even Victory must regret.
And, therefore, not too long
From the great burthen of our country's wrong
Delay our just release !
And, if it may be, save
These sacred fields of peace

From stain of patriot or of hostile blood!
Oh, help us, Lord! to roll the crimson flood
Back on its course, and, while our banners wing
Northward, strike with us! till the Goth shall cling
To his own blasted altar-stones, and crave
Mercy; and we shall grant it, and dictate
The lenient future of his fate
There, where some rotting ships and crumbling quays
Shall one day mark the Port which ruled the Western
    seas.

SPRING.

Spring, with that nameless pathos in the air
Which dwells with all things fair,
Spring, with her golden suns and silver rain,
Is with us once again.

Out in the lonely woods the jasmine burns
Its fragrant lamps, and turns
Into a royal court with green festoons
The banks of dark lagoons.

In the deep heart of every forest tree
The blood is all aglee,
And there's a look about the leafless bowers
As if they dreamed of flowers.

Yet still on every side we trace the hand
Of Winter in the land,
Save where the maple reddens on the lawn,
Flushed by the season's dawn ;

Or where, like those strange semblances we find
That age to childhood bind,
The elm puts on, as if in Nature's scorn,
The brown of Autumn corn.

As yet the turf is dark, although you know
That, not a span below,
A thousand germs are groping through the gloom,
And soon will burst their tomb.

Already, here and there, on frailest stems
Appear some azure gems,
Small as might deck, upon a gala day,
The forehead of a fay.

In gardens you may note amid the dearth
The crocus breaking earth ;
And near the snowdrop's tender white and green,
The violet in its screen.

But many gleams and shadows need must pass
Along the budding grass,
And weeks go by, before the enamored South
Shall kiss the rose's mouth.

Still there 's a sense of blossoms yet unborn
In the sweet airs of morn ;

One almost looks to see the very street
Grow purple at his feet.

At times a fragrant breeze comes floating by,
And brings, you know not why,
A feeling as when eager crowds await
Before a palace gate

Some wondrous pageant; and you scarce would start,
If from a beech's heart,
A blue-eyed Dryad, stepping forth, should say,
"Behold me! I am May!"

Ah! who would couple thoughts of war and crime
With such a blessëd time!
Who in the west wind's aromatic breath
Could hear the call of Death!

Yet not more surely shall the Spring awake
The voice of wood and brake,
Than she shall rouse, for all her tranquil charms,
A million men to arms.

There shall be deeper hues upon her plains
Than all her sunlit rains,
And every gladdening influence around,
Can summon from the ground.

Oh! standing on this desecrated mould,
Methinks that I behold,
Lifting her bloody daisies up to God,
Spring kneeling on the sod,

And calling, with the voice of all her rills,
Upon the ancient hills
To fall and crush the tyrants and the slaves
Who turn her meads to graves.

———•———

THE UNKNOWN DEAD.

The rain is plashing on my sill,
But all the winds of Heaven are still;
And so it falls with that dull sound
Which thrills us in the church-yard ground,
When the first spadeful drops like lead
Upon the coffin of the dead.
Beyond my streaming window-pane,
I cannot see the neighboring vane,
Yet from its old familiar tower
The bell comes, muffled, through the shower.
What strange and unsuspected link
Of feeling touched, has made me think—
While with a vacant soul and eye
I watch that gray and stony sky—
Of nameless graves on battle-plains
Washed by a single winter's rains,
Where, some beneath Virginian hills,
And some by green Atlantic rills,
Some by the waters of the West,
A myriad unknown heroes rest.
Ah! not the chiefs, who, dying, see

Their flags in front of victory,
Or, at their life-blood's noble cost
Pay for a battle nobly lost,
Claim from their monumental beds
The bitterest tears a nation sheds.
Beneath yon lonely mound—the spot
By all save some fond few forgot—
Lie the true martyrs of the fight
Which strikes for freedom and for right.
Of them, their patriot zeal and pride,
The lofty faith that with them died,
No grateful page shall farther tell
Than that so many bravely fell;
And we can only dimly guess
What worlds of all this world's distress,
What utter woe, despair, and dearth,
Their fate has brought to many a hearth.
Just such a sky as this should weep
Above them, always, where they sleep;
Yet, haply, at this very hour,
Their graves are like a lover's bower;
And Nature's self, with eyes unwet,
Oblivious of the crimson debt
To which she owes her April grace,
Laughs gayly o'er their burial-place.

THE TWO ARMIES.

Two armies stand enrolled beneath
The banner with the starry wreath;
One, facing battle, blight and blast,
Through twice a hundred fields has passed;
Its deeds against a ruffian foe,
Stream, valley, hill, and mountain know,
Till every wind that sweeps the land
Goes, glory laden, from the strand.

The other, with a narrower scope,
Yet led by not less grand a hope,
Hath won, perhaps, as proud a place,
And wears its fame with meeker grace.
Wives march beneath its glittering sign,
Fond mothers swell the lovely line,
And many a sweetheart hides her blush
In the young patriot's generous flush.

No breeze of battle ever fanned
The colors of that tender band;
Its office is beside the bed,
Where throbs some sick or wounded head.
It does not court the soldier's tomb,
But plies the needle and the loom;
And, by a thousand peaceful deeds,
Supplies a struggling nation's needs.

Nor is that army's gentle might
Unfelt amid the deadly fight;

It nerves the son's, the husband's hand,
It points the lover's fearless brand ;
It thrills the languid, warms the cold,
Gives even new courage to the bold ;
And sometimes lifts the veriest clod
To its own lofty trust in God.

When Heaven shall blow the trump of peace,
And bid this weary warfare cease,
Their several missions nobly done,
The triumph grasped, and freedom won,
Both armies, from their toils at rest,
Alike may claim the victor's crest,
But each shall see its dearest prize
Gleam softly from the other's eyes.

———+———

A VISION OF POESY.

PART I.

I.

In a far country, and a distant age,
    Ere sprites and fays had bade farewell to earth,
A boy was born of humble parentage ;
    The stars that shone upon his lonely birth,
Did seem to promise sovereignty and fame—
Yet no tradition hath preserved his name.

II.

'Tis said that on the night when he was born,
  A beauteous shape swept slowly through the room;
Its eyes broke on the infant like a morn,
  And his cheek brightened like a rose in bloom;
But as it passed away there followed after
A sigh of pain, and sounds of elvish laughter.

III.

And so his parents deemed him to be blest
  Beyond the lot of mortals; they were poor
As the most timid bird that stored its nest
  With the stray gleanings at their cottage-door:
Yet they contrived to rear their little dove,
And he repaid them with the tenderest love.

IV.

The child was very beautiful in sooth,
  And as he waxed in years grew lovelier still;
On his fair brow the aureole of truth
  Beamed, and the purest maidens, with a thrill,
Looked in his eyes, and from their heaven of blue
Saw thoughts like sinless Angels peering through.

V.

Need there was none of censure or of praise
  To mould him to the kind parental hand;
Yet there was ever something in his ways,
  Which those about him could not understand;
A self-withdrawn and independent bliss,
Beside the father's love, the mother's kiss.

VI.

For oft, when he believed himself alone,
  They caught brief snatches of mysterious rhymes,
Which he would murmur in an undertone,
  Like a pleased bee's in summer; and at times
A strange far look would come into his eyes,
As if he saw a vision in the skies.

VII.

And he upon a simple leaf would pore
  As if its very texture unto him
Had some deep meaning; sometimes by the door,
  From noon until a summer-day grew dim,
He lay and watched the clouds; and to his thought
Night with her stars but fitful slumbers brought.

VIII.

In the long hours of twilight, when the breeze
  Talked in low tones along the woodland rills,
Or the loud North its stormy minstrelsies
  Blent with wild noises from the distant hills,
The boy—his rosy hand against his ear
Curved like a sea-shell—hushed as some rapt seer,

IX.

Followed the sounds, and ever and again,
  As the wind came and went, in storm or play,
He seemed to hearken as to some far strain
  Of mingled voices calling him away;
And they who watched him held their breath to trace
The still and fixed attention in his face.

X.

Once, on a cold and loud-voiced winter night,
  The three were seated by their cottage-fire—
The mother watching by its flickering light
  The wakeful urchin, and the dozing sire ;
There was a brief, quick motion like a bird's,
And the boy's thought thus rippled into words:

XI.

" O mother ! thou hast taught me many things,
  But none I think more beautiful than speech—
A nobler power than even those broad wings
  I used to pray for, when I longed to reach
That distant peak which on our vale looks down,
And wears the star of evening for a crown.

XII.

" But, mother, while our human words are rife
  To us with meaning, other sounds there be
Which seem, and are, the language of a life
  Around, yet unlike ours: winds talk ; the sea
Murmurs articulately, and the sky
Listens, and answers, though inaudibly.

XIII.

" By stream and spring, in glades and woodlands lone,
  Beside our very cot, I've gathered flowers
Inscribed with signs and characters unknown ;
  But the frail scrolls still baffle all my powers :
What is this language and where is the key
That opes its weird and wondrous mystery ?

XIV.

" The forests know it, and the mountains know,
   And it is written in the sunset's dyes;
A revelation to the world below
   Is daily going on before our eyes;
And, but for sinful thoughts, I do not doubt
That we could spell the thrilling secret out.

XV.

" O mother! somewhere on this lovely earth
   I lived, and understood that mystic tongue,
But, for some reason, to my second birth
   Only the dullest memories have clung,
Like that fair tree that even while blossoming
Keeps the dead berries of a former spring.

XVI.

" Who shall put life in these?—my nightly dreams
   Some teacher of supernal powers foretell;
A fair and stately shape appears, which seems
   Bright with all truth; and once, in a dark dell
Within the forest, unto me there came
A voice that must be hers, which called my name."

XVII.

Puzzled and frightened, wondering more and more,
   The mother heard, but did not comprehend;
" So early dallying with forbidden lore!
   Oh, what will chance, and wherein will it end?
My child! my child!" she caught him to her breast,
" Oh, let me kiss these wildering thoughts to rest!

XVIII.

" They cannot come from God, who freely gives
    All that we need to have, or ought to know ;
Beware, my son ! some evil influence strives
    To grieve thy parents, and to work thee woe ;
Alas ! the vision I misunderstood !
It could not be an angel fair and good."

XIX.

And then, in low and tremulous tones, she told
    The story of his birth-night ; the boy's eyes,
As the wild tale went on, were bright and bold,
    With a weird look that did not seem surprise :
" Perhaps," he said, " this lady and her elves
Will one day come, and take me to themselves."

XX.

" And wouldst thou leave us ? " " Dearest mother, no !
    Hush ! I will check these thoughts that give thee
        pain ;
Or, if they flow, as they perchance must flow,
    At least I will not utter them again ;
Hark ! didst thou hear a voice like many streams ?
Mother ! it is the spirit of my dreams ! "

XXI.

Thenceforth, whatever impulse stirred below,
    In the deep heart beneath that childish breast,
Those lips were sealed, and though the eye would glow,
    Yet the brow wore an air of perfect rest ;

Cheerful, content, with calm though strong control
He shut the temple-portals of his soul.

XXII.

And when too restlessly the mighty throng
  Of fancies woke within his teeming mind,
All silently they formed in glorious song,
  And floated off unheard, and undivined,
Perchance not lost—with many a voiceless prayer
They reached the sky, and found some record there.

XXIII.

Softly and swiftly sped the quiet days;
  The thoughtful boy has blossomed into youth,
And still no maiden would have feared his gaze,
  And still his brow was noble with the truth :
Yet, though he masks the pain with pious art,
There burns a restless fever in his heart.

XXIV.

A childish dream is now a deathless need
  Which drives him to far hills and distant wilds ;
The solemn faith and fervor of his creed
  Bold as a martyr's, simple as a child's ;
The eagle knew him as she knew the blast,
And the deer did not flee him as he passed.

XXV.

But gentle even in his wildest mood,
  Always, and most, he loved the bluest weather,

And in some soft and sunny solitude
   Couched like a milder sunshine on the heather,
He communed with the winds, and with the birds,
As if they might have answered him in words.

XXVI.

Deep buried in the forest was a nook
   Remote and quiet as its quiet skies ;
He knew it, sought it, loved it as a book
   Full of his own sweet thoughts and memories ;
Dark oaks and fluted chestnuts gathering round,
Pillared and greenly domed a sloping mound.

XXVII.

Whereof—white, purple, azure, golden, red,
   Confused like hues of sunset—the wild flowers
Wove a rich dais ; through crosslights overhead
   Glanced the clear sunshine, fell the fruitful showers,
And here the shyest bird would fold her wings ;
Here fled the fairest and the gentlest things.

XXVIII.

Thither, one night of mist and moonlight, came
   The youth, with nothing deeper in his thoughts
Than to behold beneath the silver flame
   New aspects of his fair and favorite spot;
A single ray attained the ground, and shed
Just light enough to guide the wanderer's tread.

XXIX.

And high and hushed arose the stately trees,
    Yet shut within themselves, like dungeons, where
Lay fettered all the secrets of the breeze;
    Silent, but not as slumbering, all things there
Wore to the youth's aroused imagination
An air of deep and solemn expectation.

XXX.

" Hath Heaven," the youth exclaimed, " a sweeter spot,
    Or Earth another like it?—yet even here
The old mystery dwells! and though I read it not,
    Here most I hope—it is, or seems so near;
So many hints come to me, but, alas!
I cannot grasp the shadows as they pass.

XXXI.

" Here, from the very turf beneath me, I
    Catch, but just catch, I know not what faint sound,
And darkly guess that from yon silent sky
    Float starry emanations to the ground;
These ears are deaf, these human eyes are blind,
I want a purer heart, a subtler mind.

XXXII.

" Sometimes—could it be fancy?—I have felt
    The presence of a spirit who might speak;
As down in lowly reverence I knelt
    Its very breath hath kissed my burning cheek;

7

But I in vain have hushed my own to heai
A wing or whisper stir the silent air!"

XXXIII.

Is not the breeze articulate?   Hark! Oh, hark!
    A distant murmur, like a voice of floods;
And onward sweeping slowly through the dark,
    Bursts like a call the night-wind from the woods!
Low bow the flowers, the trees fling loose their dreams.
And through the waving roof a fresher moonlight
        streams.

XXXIV.

" Mortal! "—the word crept slowly round the place
    As if that wind had breathed it!   From no star
Streams that soft lustre on the dreamer's face.
    Again a hushing calm! while faint and far
The breeze goes calling onward through the night.
Dear God! what vision chains that wide-strained sight?

XXXV.

Over the grass and flowers, and up the slope
    Glides a white cloud of mist, self-moved and slow,
That, pausing at the hillock's moonlit cope,
    Swayed like a flame of silver; from below
The breathless youth with beating heart beholds
A mystic motion in its argent folds.

XXXVI.

Yet his young soul is bold, and hope grows warm,
    As flashing through that cloud of shadowy crape,

With sweep of robes, and then a gleaming arm,
   Slowly developing, at last took shape
A face and form unutterably bright,
That cast a golden glamour on the night.

XXXVII.

But for the glory round it it would seem
   Almost a mortal maiden; and the boy,
Unto whom love was yet an innocent dream,
   Shivered and crimsoned with an unknown joy;
As to the young Spring bounds the passionate South,
He could have clasped and kissed her mouth to mouth.

XXXVIII.

Yet something checked, that was and was not dread,
   Till in a low sweet voice the maiden spake;
She was the Fairy of his dreams, she said,
   And loved him simply for his human sake;
And that in heaven, wherefrom she took her birth,
They called her Poesy, the angel of the earth.

XXXIX.

" And ever since that immemorial hour,
   When the glad morning-stars together sung,
My task hath been, beneath a mightier Power,
   To keep the world forever fresh and young;
I give it not its fruitage and its green,
But clothe it with a glory all unseen.

XL.

" I sow the germ which buds in human art,
    And, with my sister, Science, I explore
With light the dark recesses of the heart,
    And nerve the will, and teach the wish to soar;
I touch with grace the body's meanest clay,
While noble souls are nobler for my sway.

XLI.

" Before my power the kings of earth have bowed;
    I am the voice of Freedom, and the sword
Leaps from its scabbard when I call aloud ;
    Wherever life in sacrifice is poured,
Wherever martyrs die or patriots bleed,
I weave the chaplet and award the meed.

XLII.

" Where Passion stoops, or strays, is cold, or dead,
    I lift from error, or to action thrill !
Or if it rage too madly in its bed,
    The tempest hushes at my 'peace ! be still !'
I know how far its tides should sink or swell,
And they obey my sceptre and my spell.

XLIII.

" All lovely things, and gentle—the sweet laugh
Of children, Girlhood's kiss, and Friendship's clasp,
The boy that sporteth with the old man's staff,
    The baby, and the breast its fingers grasp—

All that exalts the grounds of happiness,
All griefs that hallow, and all joys that bless,

XLIV.

" To me are sacred ; at my holy shrine
   Love breathes its latest dreams, its earliest hints ;
I turn life's tasteless waters into wine,
     And flush them through and through with purple
       tints.
Wherever Earth is fair, and Heaven looks down,
I rear my altars, and I wear my crown.

XLV.

" I am the unseen spirit thou hast sought,
   I woke those shadowy questionings that vex
Thy young mind, lost in its own cloud of thought,
     And rouse the soul they trouble and perplex ;
I filled thy days with visions, and thy nights
Blessed with all sweetest sounds and fairy sights.

XLVI.

" Not here, not in this world, may I disclose
   The mysteries in which this life is hearsed ;
Some doubts there be that, with some earthly woes,
     By Death alone shall wholly be dispersed ;
Yet on those very doubts from this low sod
Thy soul shall pass beyond the stars to God.

XLVII.

" And so to knowledge, climbing grade by grade,
   Thou shalt attain whatever mortals can,

And what thou mayst discover by my aid
  Thou shalt translate unto thy brother man ;
And men shall bless the power that flings a ray
Into their night from thy diviner day.

XLVIII.

" For, from thy lofty height, thy words shall fall
  Upon their spirits like bright cataracts
That front a sunrise ; thou shalt hear them call
  Amid their endless waste of arid facts,
As wearily they plod their way along,
Upon the rhythmic zephyrs of thy song.

XLIX.

"All this is in thy reach, but much depends
  Upon thyself—thy future I await ;
I give the genius, point the proper ends,
  But the true bard is his own only Fate ;
Into thy soul my soul have I infused ;
Take care thy lofty powers be wisely used.

L.

" The Poet owes a high and holy debt,
  Which, if he feel, he craves not to be heard
For the poor boon of praise, or place, nor yet
  Does the mere joy of song, as with the bird
Of many voices, prompt the choral lay
That cheers that gentle pilgrim on his way.

LI.

" Nor may he always sweep the passionate lyre,
    Which is his heart, only for such relief
As an impatient spirit may desire,
    Lest, from the grave which hides a private grief,
The spells of song call up some pallid wraith
To blast or ban a mortal hope or faith.

LII.

" Yet over his deep soul, with all its crowd
    Of varying hopes and fears, he still must brood;
As from its azure height a tranquil cloud
    Watches its own bright changes in the flood ;
Self-reading, not self-loving—they are twain—
And sounding, while he mourns, the depths of pain.

LIII.

" Thus shall his songs attain the common breast,
    Dyed in his own life's blood, the sign and seal,
Even as the thorns which are the martyr's crest,
    That do attest his office, and appeal
Unto the universal human heart
In sanction of his mission and his art.

LIV.

" Much yet remains unsaid—pure must he be ;
    Oh, blessèd are the pure! for they shall hear
Where others hear not, see where others see
    With a dazed vision : who have drawn most near
My shrine, have ever brought a spirit cased
And mailèd in a body clean and chaste.

LV.

" The Poet to the whole wide world belongs,
    Even as the teacher is the child's—I said
No selfish aim should ever mar his songs,
    But self wears many guises; men may wed
Self in another, and the soul may be
Self to its centre, all unconsciously.

LVI.

" And therefore must the Poet watch, lest he,
    In the dark struggle of this life, should take
Stains which he might not notice; he must flee
    Falsehood, however winsome, and forsake
All for the Truth, assured that Truth alone
Is Beauty, and can make him all my own.

LVII.

" And he must be as arméd warrior strong,
    And he must be as gentle as a girl,
And he must front, and sometimes suffer wrong,
    With brow unbent, and lip untaught to curl;
For wrath, and scorn, and pride, however just,
Fill the clear spirit's eyes with earthly dust."

The story came to me—it recks not whence—
In fragments; Oh! if I could tell it all,
If human speech indeed could tell it all,
'T were not a whit less wondrous, than if I
Should find, untouched in leaf and stem, and bright
As when it bloomed three thousand years ago,

On some Idalian slope, a perfect rose.
Alas! a leaf or two, and they perchance
Scarce worth the hiving, one or two dead leaves
Are the sole harvest of a summer's toil.
There was a moment, ne'er to be recalled,
When to the Poet's hope within my heart,
They wore a tint like life's, but in my hand,
I know not why, they withered.   I have heard
Somewhere, of some dead monarch, from the tomb,
Where he had slept a century and more,
Brought forth, that when the coffin was laid bare,
Albeit the body in its mouldering robes
Was fleshless, yet one feature still remained
Perfect, or perfect seemed at least; the eyes
Gleamed for a second on the startled crowd,
And then went out in ashes.   Even thus
The story, when I drew it from the grave
Where it had lain so long, did seem, I thought,
Not wholly lifeless; but even while I gazed
To fix its features on my heart, and called
The world to wonder with me, lo! it proved
I looked upon a corpse!
                                        What further fell
In that lone forest nook, how much was taught,
How much was only hinted, what the youth
Promised, if promise were required, to do
Or strive for, what the gifts he bore away—
Or added powers or blessings—how at last,
The vision ended and he sought his home,
How lived there, and how long, and when he passed

Into the busy world to seek his fate,
I know not, and if any ever knew,
The tale hath perished from the earth; for here
The slender thread on which my song is strung
Breaks off, and many after-years of life
Are lost to sight, the life to reappear
Only towards its close—as of a dream
We catch the end and opening, but forget
That which had joined them in the dreaming brain;
Or as a mountain with a belt of mist
That shows his base, and far above, a peak
With a blue plume of pines.
                              But turn the page
And read the only hints that yet remain.

Part II.

I.

It is not winter yet, but that sweet time
  In autumn when the first cool days are past;
A week ago, the leaves were hoar with rime,
    And some have dropped before the North wind's
      blast;
But the mild hours are back, and at mid-noon,
The day hath all the genial warmth of June.

II.

What slender form lies stretched along the mound?
  Can it be his, the Wanderer's, with that brow

Gray in its prime, those eyes that wander round
　　Listlessly, with a jaded glance that now
Seems to see nothing where it rests, and then
Pores on each trivial object in its ken?

III.

See how a gentle maid's wan fingers clasp
　　The last fond love-notes of some faithless hand;
Thus, with a transient interest, his weak grasp
　　Holds a few leaves as when of old he scanned
The meaning in their gold and crimson streaks,
But the sweet dream has vanished! hush! he speaks!

IV.

" Once more, once more, after long pain and toil,
　　And yet not long, if I should count by years,
I breathe my native air, and tread the soil
　　I trod in childhood; if I shed no tears,
No happy tears, 't is that their fount is dry,
And joy that cannot weep must sigh, must sigh.

V.

" These leaves, my boyish books in days of yore,
　　When, as the weeks sped by, I seemed to stand
Ever upon the brink of some wild lore—
　　These leaves shall make my bed, and—for the hand
Of God is on me, chilling brain and breath—
I shall not ask a softer couch in death.

VI.

" Here was it that I saw, or dreamed I saw,
   I know not which, that shape of love and light.
Spirit of Song! have I not owned thy law?
   Have I not taught, or striven to teach the right,
And kept my heart as clean, my life as sweet,
As mortals may, when mortals mortals meet?

VII.

" Thou knowst how I went forth, my youthful breast
   On fire with thee, amid the paths of men;
Once in my wanderings, my lone footsteps pressed
   A mountain forest; in a sombre glen,
Down which its thunderous boom a cataract flung,
A little bird, unheeded, built and sung.

VIII.

"So fell my voice amid the whirl and rush
   Of human passions; if unto my art
Sorrow hath sometimes owed a gentler gush,
   I know it not; if any Poet-heart
Hath kindled at my songs its light divine,
I know it not; no ray came back to mine.

IX.

" Alone in crowds, once more I sought to make
   Of senseless things my friends; the clouds that burn
Above the sunset, and the flowers that shake
   Their odors in the wind—these would not turn

Their faces from me; far from cities, I
Forgot the scornful world that passed me by.

X.

" Yet even the world's cold slights I might have borne,
　　Nor fled, though sorrowing; but I shrank at last
When one sweet face, too sweet, I thought, for scorn,
　　Looked scornfully upon me; then I passed
From all that youth had dreamed or manhood planned,
Into the self that none would understand.

XI.

" She was—I never wronged her womanhood
　　By crowning it with praises not her own—
She was all earth's, and earth's, too, in that mood
　　When she brings forth her fairest; I atone
Now, in this fading brow and failing frame,
That such a soul such soul as mine could tame.

XII.

" Clay to its kindred clay! I loved, in sooth,
　　Too deeply and too purely to be blest;
With something more of lust and less of truth
　　She would have sunk all blushes on my breast,
And—but I must not blame her—in my ear
Death whispers! and the end, thank God! draws
　　　　near!"

XIII.

Hist! on the perfect silence of the place
　　Comes and dies off a sound like far-off rain

With voices mingled ; on the Poet's face
  A shadow, where no shadow should have lain,
Falls the next moment: nothing meets his sight,
Yet something moves betwixt him and the light.

XIV.

And a voice murmurs, " Wonder not, but hear !
  ME to behold again thou need'st not seek ;
Yet by the dim-felt influence on the air,
  And by the mystic shadow on thy cheek,
Know, though thou mayst not touch with **fleshly**
      hands,
The genius of thy life beside thee stands !

XV.

" Unto no fault, O weary-hearted one !
  Unto no fault of man's thou ow'st thy fate ;
All human hearts that beat this earth upon,
  All human thoughts and human passions wait
Upon the genuine bard, to him belong,
And help in their own way the Poet's song.

XVI.

"How blame the world ? for the world hast **thou**
      wrought ?
  Or wast thou but as one who aims to fling
The weight of some unutterable thought
  Down like a burden ? what from questioning
Too subtly thy own spirit, and to speech
But half subduing themes beyond the reach

XVII.

" Of mortal reason ; what from living much
   In that dark world of shadows, where the soul
Wanders bewildered, striving still to clutch,
   Yet never clutching once, a shadowy goal,
Which always flies, and while it flies seems near,
Thy songs were riddles hard to mortal ear.

XVIII.

" This was the hidden selfishness that marred
   Thy teachings ever; this the false key-note
That on such souls as might have loved thee jarred
   Like an unearthly language ; thou didst float
On a strange water; those who stood on land
Gazed, but they could not leave their beaten strand.

XIX.

" Your elements were different, and apart—
   The world's and thine—and even in those intense
And watchful broodings o'er thy inmost heart,
   It was thy own peculiar difference
That thou didst seek ; nor didst thou care to find
Aught that would bring thee nearer to thy kind.

XX.

" Not thus the Poet, who in blood and brain
   Would represent his race and speak for all,
Weaves the bright woof of that impassioned strain
   Which drapes, as if for some high festival
Of pure delights—whence few of human birth
May rightly be shut out—the common earth.

XXI.

" As the same law that moulds a planet, rounds
    A drop of dew, so the great Poet spheres
Worlds in himself; no selfish limit bounds
    A sympathy that folds all characters,
All ranks, all passions, and all life almost
In its wide circle.   Like some noble host,

XXII.

" He spreads the riches of his soul, and bids
    Partake who will.   Age has its saws of truth,
And love is for the maiden's drooping lids,
    And words of passion for the earnest youth ;
Wisdom for all ; and when it seeks relief,
Tears, and their solace for the heart of grief.

XXIII.

" Nor less on him than thee the mysteries
    Within him and about him ever weigh—
The meanings in the stars, and in the breeze,
    All the weird wonders of the common day,
Truths that the merest point removes from reach,
And thoughts that pause upon the brink of speech ;

XXIV.

" But on the surface of his song these lie
    As shadows, not as darkness ; and alway,
Even though it breathe the secrets of the sky,
    There is a human purpose in the lay ;
Thus some tall fir that whispers to the stars
Shields at its base a cotter's lattice-bars.

XXV.

" Even such my Poet! for thou still art mine!
   Thou mightst have been, and now have calmly died,
A priest, and not a victim at the shrine;
   Alas! yet was it all thy fault? I chide,
Perchance, myself within thee, and the fate
To which thy power was solely consecrate.

XXVI.

" Thy life hath not been wholly without use,
   Albeit that use is partly hidden now;
In thy unmingled scorn of any truce
   With this world's specious falsehoods, often thou
Hast uttered, through some all unworldly song,
Truths that for man might else have slumbered long.

XXVII.

" And these not always vainly on the crowd
   Have fallen; some are cherished now, and some,
In mystic phrases wrapped as in a shroud,
   Wait the diviner, who as yet is dumb
Upon the breast of God—the gate of birth
Closed on a dreamless ignorance of earth.

XXVIII.

" And therefore, though thy name shall pass away,
   Even as a cloud that hath wept all its showers,
Yet as that cloud shall live again one day
   In the glad grass, and in the happy flowers,
So in thy thoughts, though clothed in sweeter rhymes,
Thy life shall bear its flowers in future times."

THE PAST.

To-day's most trivial act may hold the seed
  Of future fruitfulness, or future dearth ;
Oh, cherish always every word and deed!
  The simplest record of thyself hath worth.

If thou hast ever slighted one old thought,
  Beware lest Grief enforce the truth at last;
The time must come wherein thou shalt be taught
  The value and the beauty of the Past.

Not merely as a warner and a guide,
  "A voice behind thee," sounding to the strife ;
But something never to be put aside,
  A part and parcel of thy present life.

Not as a distant and a darkened sky,
  Through which the stars peep, and the moonbeams
      glow ;
But a surrounding atmosphere, whereby
  We live and breathe, sustained in pain and woe.

A shadowy land, where joy and sorrow kiss,
  Each still to each corrective and relief,
Where dim delights are brightened into bliss,
  And nothing wholly perishes but Grief.

Ah, me!—not dies—no more than spirit dies ;
  But in a change like death is clothed with wings ;
A serious angel, with entrancëd eyes,
  Looking to far-off and celestial things.

PRÆCEPTOR AMAT.

It is time (it was time long ago) I should sever
This chain—why I wear it I know not—forever!
Yet I cling to the bond, even while sick of the mask
I must wear, as of one whom his commonplace task
And proof-armorofdullnesshave steeled to her charms!
Ah! how lovely she looked as she flung from her arms,
In heaps to this table (now starred with the stains
Of her booty yet wet with those yesterday rains),
These roses and lilies, and—what? let me see!
Then was off in a moment, but turned with a glee,
That lit her sweet face as with moonlight, to say,
As 't was almost too late for a lesson to-day,
She meant to usurp, for this morning at least,
My office of Tutor; and instead of a feast
Of such mouthfuls as *poluphloisboio thalasses*,
With which I fed her, I should study the grasses
(Love-grasses she called them), the buds, and the
            flowers
Of which I know nothing; and if " with *my* powers,"
I did not learn all she could teach in that time,
And thank her, perhaps, in a sweet English rhyme,
If I did not do this, and she flung back her hair,
And shook her bright head with a menacing air,
She'd be—oh! she'd be—a real Saracen Omar
To a certain much-valued edition of Homer!
But these flowers! I believe I could number as soon
The shadowy thoughts of a last summer's noon,

Or recall with their phases, each one after one,
The clouds that came down to the death of the Sun.
Cirrus, Stratus, or Nimbus, some evening last year,
As unravel the web of one genus!   Why, there,
As they lie by my desk in that glistering heap,
All tangled together like dreams in the sleep
Of a bliss-fevered heart, I might turn them and turn
Till night, in a puzzle of pleasure, and learn
Not a fact, not a secret I prize half so much,
As, how rough is this leaf when I think of her touch.
There's one now blown yonder! what can be its name?
A topaz wine-colored, the wine in a flame ;
And another that's hued like the pulp of a melon,
But sprinkled all o'er with seed-pearls of Ceylon ;
And a third! its white petals just clouded with pink!
And a fourth, that blue star! and then this, too! I
      think
If one brought me this moment an amethyst cup,
From which, through a liquor of amber, looked up,
With a glow as of eyes in their elfin-like lustre,
Stones culled from all lands in a sunshiny cluster,
From the ruby that burns in the sands of Mysore
To the beryl of Daunia, with gems from the core
Of the mountains of Persia (I talk like a boy
In the flush of some new, and yet half-tasted joy) ;
But I think if that cup and its jewels together
Were placed by the side of this child of the weather
(This one which she touched with her mouth, and let
      slip
From her fingers by chance, as her exquisite lip,

With a music befitting the language divine,
Gave the roll of the Greek's multitudinous line),
I should take—not the gems—but enough! let me
    shut
In the blossom that woke it, my folly, and put
Both away in my bosom—there, in a heart-niche,
One shall outlive the other—is 't hard to tell which?
In the name of all starry and beautiful things,
What is it? the cross in the centre, these rings,
And the petals that shoot in an intricate maze,
From the disk which is lilac—or purple? like rays
In a blue Aureole!

                And so now will she wot,
When I sit by her side with my brows in a knot,
And praise her so calmly, or chide her perhaps,
If her voice falter once in its musical lapse,
As I've done, I confess, just to gaze at a flush
In the white of her throat, or to watch the quick rush
Of the tear she sheds smiling, as, drooping her curls
O'er that book I keep shrined like a casket of pearls.
She reads on in low tones of such tremulous sweetness,
That (in spite of some faults) I am forced, in discreet-
    ness,
To silence, lest mine, growing hoarse, should betray
What I must not reveal—will she guess now, I say,
How, for all his grave looks, the stern, passionless
    Tutor,
With more than the love of her youthfulest suitor.

Is hiding somewhere in the shroud of his vest,
By a heart that is beating wild wings in its nest,
This flower, thrown aside in the sport of a minute,
And which he holds dear as though folded within it
Lay the germ of the bliss that he dreams of! Ah, me!
It is hard to love thus, yet to seem and to be
A thing for indifference, faint praise, or cold blame,
When you long (by the right of deep passion, the claim,
On the loved of the loving, at least to be heard)
To take the white hand, and with glance, touch, and
  word,
Burn your way to the heart! That her step on the
  stair?
Be still thou fond flutterer!

                        How little I care
For your favorites, see! they are all of them, look!
On the spot where they fell, and—but here is your
  book!

DREAMS.

Who first said "false as dreams?" Not one who saw
  Into the wild and wondrous world they sway;
No thinker who hath read their mystic law;
  No Poet who hath weaved them in his lay.

Else had he known that through the human breast
  Cross and recross a thousand fleeting gleams,

That, passed unnoticed in the day's unrest,
  Come out at night, like stars, in shining dreams;

That minds too busy or too dull to mark
  The dim suggestion of the noisier hours,
By dreams in the deep silence of the dark,
  Are roused at midnight with their folded powers.

Like that old fount beneath Dodona's oaks,
  That, dry and voiceless in the garish noon,
When the calm night arose with modest looks,
  Caught with full wave the sparkle of the moon.

If, now and then, a ghastly shape glide in,
  And fright us with its horrid gloom or glee,
It is the ghost of some forgotten sin
  We failed to exorcise on bended knee.

And that sweet face which only yesternight
  Came to thy solace, dreamer (didst thou read
The blessing in its eyes of tearful light?)
  Was but the spirit of some gentle deed.

Each has its lesson; for our dreams in sooth,
  Come they in shape of demons, gods, or elve
Are allegories with deep hearts of truth
  That tell us solemn secrets of ourselves.

THE PROBLEM.

Not to win thy favor, maiden, not to steal away thy
    heart,
Have I ever sought thy presence, ever stooped to any
    art ;
Thou wast but a wildering problem, which I aimed to
    solve, and then
Make it matter for my note-book, or a picture for my
    pen.
So, I daily conned thee over, thinking it no dangerous
    task,
Peeping underneath thy lashes, peering underneath
    thy mask—
For thou wear'st one—no denial! there is much with-
    in thine eyes;
But those stars have other secrets than are patent in
    their skies.
And I read thee, read thee closely, every grace and
    every sin,
Looked behind the outward seeming to the strange
    wild world within,
Where thy future self is forming, where I saw—no
    matter what !
There was something less than angel, there was many
    an earthly spot ;
Yet so beautiful thy errors that I had no heart for
    blame,
And thy virtues made thee dearer than my dearest
    hopes of fame ;

All so blended, that in wishing one peculiar trait
    removed,
We indeed might make thee better, but less lovely
    and less loved.
All my mind was in the study—so two thrilling fort-
    nights passed—
All my mind was in the study—till my heart was
    touched at last.
Well! and then the book was finished, the absorbing
    task was done,
I awoke as one who had been dreaming in a noonday
    sun ;
With a fever on my forehead, and a throbbing in my
    brain,
In my soul delirious wishes, in my heart a lasting
    pain ;
Yet so hopeless, yet so cureless—as in every great
    despair—
I was very calm and silent, and I never stooped to
    prayer,
Like a sick man unattended, reckless of the coming
    death,
Only for he knows it certain, and he feels no sister's
    breath.
All the while as by an Até, with no pity in her face,
Yet with eyes of witching beauty, and with form of
    matchless grace,
I was haunted by thy presence, oh! for weary nights
    and days,
I was haunted by thy spirit, I was troubled by thy gaze,

And the question which to answer I had taxed a
    subtle brain,
What thou art, and what thou wilt be, came again
    and yet again ;
With its opposite deductions, it recurred a thousand
    times,
Like a coward's apprehensions, like a madman's favor-
    ite rhymes.
But to-night my thoughts flow calmer—in thy room
    I think I stand,
See a fair white page before thee, and a pen within thy
    hand ;
And thy fingers sweep the paper, and a light is in
    thine eyes,
Whilst I read thy secret fancies, whilst I hear thy
    secret sighs.
What they are I will not whisper, those are lovely,
    these are deep,
But one name is left unwritten, that is only breathed
    in sleep.
Is it wonder that my passion bursts at once from out
    its nest ?
I have bent my knee before thee, and my love is all
    confessed ;
Though I knew that name unwritten was another
    name than mine,
Though I felt those sighs half murmured what I could
    but half divine.
Aye! I hear thy haughty answer! Aye! I see thy
    proud lip curl!

"What presumption, and what folly!" why, I only
    love a girl
With some very winning graces, with some very noble
    traits,
But no better than a thousand who have bent to
    humbler fates.
That I ask not; I have, maiden, just as haught a soul
    as thine;
If thou think'st thy place above me, thou shalt never
    stoop to mine.
Yet as long as blood runs redly, yet as long as mental
    worth
Is a nobler gift than fortune, is a holier thing than birth,
I will claim the right to utter, to the high and to the
    low,
That I love them, or I hate them, that I am a friend
    or foe.
Nor shall any slight unman me; I have yet some
    little strength.
Yet my song shall sound as sweetly, yet a power be
    mine at length!
Then, oh, then! but moans are idle—hear me, pitying
    saints above!
With a chaplet on my forehead, I will justify my love.
And perhaps when thou art leaning on some less
    devoted breast,
Thou shalt murmur, "He was worthier than my
    blinded spirit guessed."

THE ARCTIC VOYAGER.

Shall I desist, twice baffled ?   Once by land,
And once by sea, I fought and strove with storms,
All shades of danger, tides, and weary calms ;
Head-currents, cold and famine, savage beasts,
And men more savage; all the while my face
Looked northward toward the pole ; if mortal strength
Could have sustained me, I had never turned
Till I had seen the star which never sets
Freeze in the Arctic zenith.   That I failed
To solve the mysteries of the ice-bound world,
Was not because I faltered in the quest.
Witness those pathless forests which conceal
The bones of perished comrades, that long march,
Blood-tracked o'er flint and snow, and one dread night
By Athabasca, when a cherished life
Flowed to give life to others.   This, and worse,
I suffered—let it pass—it has not tamed
My spirit nor the faith which was my strength.
Despite of waning years, despite the world
Which doubts, the few who dare, I purpose now—
A purpose long and thoughtfully resolved,
Through all its grounds of reasonable hope—
To seek beyond the ice which guards the Pole,
A sea of open water ; for I hold,
Not without proofs, that such a sea exists,
And may be reached, though since this earth was made
No keel hath ploughed it, and to mortal ear

No wind hath told its secrets . . . . With this tide
I sail; if all be well, this very moon
Shall see my ship beyond the southern cape
Of Greenland, and far up the bay through which,
With diamond spire and gorgeous pinnacle,
The fleets of winter pass to warmer seas.
Whether, my hardy shipmates! we shall reach
Our bourne, and come with tales of wonder back,
Or whether we shall lose the precious time,
Locked in thick ice, or whether some strange fate
Shall end us all, I know not; but I know
A lofty hope, if earnestly pursued,
Is its own crown, and never in this life
Is labor wholly fruitless.   In this faith
I shall not count the chances—sure that all
A prudent foresight asks we shall not want,
And all that bold and patient hearts can do
Ye will not leave undone.   The rest is God's!

———◆———

A YEAR'S COURTSHIP.

I saw her, Harry, first, in March—
   You know the street that leadeth down
By the old bridge's crumbling arch ?—
   Just where it leaves the dusty town

A lonely house stands grim and dark—
   You've seen it? then I need not say

How quaint the place is—did you mark
  An ivied window ? well! one day,

I, chasing some forgotten dream,
  And in a poet's idlest mood,
Caught, as I passed, a white hand's gleam—
  A shutter opened—there she stood

Training the ivy to its prop.
  Two dark eyes and a brow of snow
Flashed down upon me—did I stop ?—
  She says I did—I do not know.

But all that day did something glow
  Just where the heart beats; frail and slight,
A germ had slipped its shell, and now
  Was pushing softly for the light.

And April saw me at her feet,
  Dear month of sunshine and of rain !
My very fears were sometimes sweet,
  And hope was often touched with pain.

For she was frank, and she was coy,
  A willful April in her ways;
And in a dream of doubtful joy
  I passed some truly April days.

May came, and on that arch, sweet mouth,
  The smile was graver in its play,
And, softening with the softening South,
  My April melted into May.

She loved me, yet my heart would doubt,
   And ere I spoke the month was June—
One warm still night we wandered out
   To watch a slowly setting moon.

Something which I saw not—my eyes
   Were not on heaven—a star, perchance,
Or some bright drapery of the skies,
   Had caught her earnest, upper glance.

And as she paused—Hal! we have played
   Upon the very spot—a fir
Just touched me with its dreamy shade,
   But the full moonlight fell on her—

And as she paused—I know not why—
   I longed to speak, yet could not speak ;
The bashful are the boldest—I—
   I stooped and gently kissed her cheek.

A murmur (else some fragrant air
   Stirred softly) and the faintest start—
O Hal ! we were the happiest pair !
   O Hal! I clasped her heart to heart!

And kissed away some tears that gushed ;
   But how she trembled, timid dove,
When my soul broke its silence, flushed
   With a whole burning June of love.

Since then a happy year hath sped
   Through months that seemed all June and May,

And soon a March sun, overhead,
  Will usher in the crowning day.

Twelve blessed moons that seemed to glow
  All summer, Hal!—my peerless Kate!
She is the dearest—" Angel ? "—no !
  Thank God !—but you shall see her—wait.

So all is told ! I count on thee
  To see the Priest, Hal !   Pass the wine !
Here's to my darling wife to be !
  And here's to—when thou find'st her—thine !

———•———

DRAMATIC FRAGMENT.

Let the boy have his will ! I tell thee, brother,
We treat these little ones too much like flowers,
Training them, in blind selfishness, to deck
Sticks of our poor setting, when they might,
If left to clamber where themselves incline,
Find nobler props to cling to, fitter place,
And sweeter air to bloom in.   It is wrong—
Thou striv'st to sow with feelings all thine own,
With thoughts and hopes, anxieties and aims,
Born of thine own peculiar self, and fed
Upon a certain round of circumstance,
A soul as different and distinct from thine
As love of goodness is from love of glory,
Or noble poesy from noble prose.

I could forgive thee, if thou wast of them
Who do their fated parts in this world's business,
Scarce knowing how or why—for common minds
See not the difference 'twixt themselves and others—
But thou, thou, with the visions which thy youth did
      cherish
Substantialized upon thy regal brow,
Shouldst boast a deeper insight. We are born,
It is my faith, in miniature completeness,
And like each other only in our weakness.
Even with our mother's milk upon our lips,
Our smiles have different meanings, and our hands
Press with degrees of softness to her bosom.
It is not change—whatever in the heart
That wears its semblance, we, in looking back,
With gratulation or regret, perceive—
It is not change we undergo, but only
Growth or development. Yes! what is childhood
But after all a sort of golden daylight,
A beautiful and blessed wealth of sunshine.
Wherein the powers and passions of the soul
Sleep starlike but existent, till the night
Of gathering years shall call the slumbers forth,
And they rise up in glory ? Early grief,
A shadow like the darkness of eclipse,
Hath sometimes waked them sooner.

THE SUMMER BOWER.

It is a place whither I've often gone
For peace, and found it, secret, hushed, and cool,
A beautiful recess in neighboring woods.
Trees of the soberest hues, thick-leaved and tall,
Arch it o'erhead and column it around,
Framing a covert, natural and wild,
Domelike and dim ; though nowhere so enclosed
But that the gentlest breezes reach the spot
Unwearied and unweakened.   Sound is here
A transient and unfrequent visitor ;
Yet if the day be calm, not often then,
Whilst the high pines in one another's arms
Sleep, you may sometimes with unstartled ear
Catch the far fall of voices, how remote
You know not, and you do not care to know.
The turf is soft and green, but not a flower
Lights the recess, save one, star-shaped and bright—
I do not know its name—which here and there
Gleams like a sapphire set in emerald.
A narrow opening in the branchëd roof,
A single one, is large enough to show,
With that half glimpse a dreamer loves so much,
The blue air and the blessing of the sky.
Thither I always bent my idle steps,
When griefs depressed, or joys disturbed my heart,
And found the calm I looked for, or returned
Strong with the quiet rapture in my soul.

But one day,
One of those July days when winds have fled
One knows not whither, I, most sick in mind
With thoughts that shall be nameless, yet, no doubt,
Wrong, or at least unhealthful, since though dark
With gloom, and touched with discontent, they had
No adequate excuse, nor cause, nor end,
I, with these thoughts, and on this summer day,
Entered the accustomed haunt, and found for once
No medicinal virtue.
            Not a leaf
Stirred with the whispering welcome which I sought,
But in a close and humid atmosphere,
Every fair plant and implicated bough
Hung lax and lifeless. Something in the place,
Its utter stillness, the unusual heat,
And some more secret influence, I thought,
Weighed on the sense like sin. Above I saw,
Though not a cloud was visible in heaven,
The pallid sky look through a glazèd mist
Like a blue·eye in death.
              The change, perhaps,
Was natural enough ; my jaundiced sight,
The weather, and the time explain it all :
Yet have I drawn a lesson from the spot,
And shrined it in these verses for my heart.
Thenceforth those tranquil precincts I have sought
Not less, and in all shades of various moods ;
But always shun to desecrate the spot
By vain repinings, sickly sentiments,

Or inconclusive sorrows.   Nature, though
Pure as she was in Eden when her breath
Kissed the white brow of Eve, doth not refuse,
In her own way and with a just reserve,
To sympathize with human suffering;
But for the pains, the fever, and the fret
Engendered of a weak, unquiet heart,
She hath no solace; and who seeks her when
These be the troubles over which he moans,
Reads in her unreplying lineaments
Rebukes, that, to the guilty consciousness,
Strike like contempt.

A RHAPSODY OF A SOUTHERN WINTER NIGHT.

Oh! dost thou flatter falsely, Hope?
The day hath scarcely passed that saw thy birth,
Yet thy white wings are plumed to all their scope,
And hour by hour thine eyes have gathered light,
    And grown so large and bright,
That my whole future life unfolds what seems,
    Beneath their gentle beams,
A path that leads athwart some guiltless earth,
To which a star is dropping from the night!

      Not many moons ago,
But when these leafless beds were all aglow
With summer's dearest treasures, I

Was reading in this lonely garden-nook;
A July noon was cloudless in the sky,
And soon I put my shallow studies by;
Then, sick at heart, and angered by the book,
Which, in good sooth, was but the long-drawn sigh
Of some one who had quarrelled with his kind,
Vexed at the very proofs which I had sought,
And all annoyed while all alert to find
A plausible likeness of my own dark thought,
I cast me down beneath yon oak's wide boughs,
And, shielding with both hands my throbbing brows,
Watched lazily the shadows of my brain.
The feeble tide of peevishness went down,
And left a flat dull waste of dreary pain,
Which seemed to clog the blood in every vein;
The world, of course, put on its darkest frown—
In all its realms I saw no mortal crown
Which did not wound or crush some restless head;
And hope, and will, and motive, all were dead.
So, passive as a stone, I felt too low
To claim a kindred with the humblest flower;
Even that would bare its bosom to a shower,
While I henceforth would take no pains to live,
Nor place myself where I might feel or give
A single impulse whence a wish could grow.
There was a tulip scarce a gossamer's throw
Beyond that platanus. A little child,
Most dear to me, looked through the fence and smiled
A hint that I should pluck it for her sake.
Ah, me! I trust I was not well awake—

The voice was very sweet,
Yet a faint languor kept me in my seat.
I saw a pouted lip, a toss, and heard
Some low expostulating tones, but stirred
Not even a leaf's length, till the pretty fay,
Wondering, and half abashed at the wild feat,
Climbed the low pales, and laughed my gloom **away.**

And here again, but led by other powers,
A morning and a golden afternoon,
These happy stars, and yonder setting moon,
Have seen me speed, unreckoned and untasked,
          A round of precious hours.
Oh! here, where in that summer noon I basked,
And strove, with logic frailer than the flowers,
To justify a life of sensuous rest,
A question dear as home or heaven was asked,
And without language answered.   I was blest!
Blest with those nameless boons too sweet to trust
Unto the telltale confidence of song.
Love to his own glad self is sometimes coy,
And even thus much doth seem to do him wrong;
While in the fears which chasten mortal joy,
Is one that shuts the lips, lest speech too free,
With the cold touch of hard reality,
Should turn its priceless jewels into dust.
Since that long kiss which closed the morning's **talk,**.
I have not strayed beyond this garden walk.
As yet a vague delight is all I know,
A sense of joy so wild 'tis almost pain,

And like a trouble drives me to and fro,
And will not pause to count its own sweet gain.
I am so happy! that is all my thought.
To-morrow I will turn it round and round,
And seek to know its limits and its ground.
To-morrow I will task my heart to learn
The duties which shall spring from such a seed,
And where it must be sown, and how be wrought.
But oh! this reckless bliss is bliss indeed!
And for one day I choose to seal the urn
Wherein is shrined Love's missal and his creed.
Meantime I give my fancy all it craves;
Like him who found the West when first he caught
The light that glittered from the world he sought,
And furled his sails till Dawn should show the land;
While in glad dreams he saw the ambient waves
Go rippling brightly up a golden strand.

Hath there not been a softer breath at play
In the long woodland aisles than often sweeps
At this rough season through their solemn deeps—
A gentle Ariel sent by gentle May,
　　　Who knew it was the morn
　　　On which a hope was born,
To greet the flower ere it was fully blown,
And nurse it as some lily of her own?
And wherefore, save to grace a happy day,
Did the whole West at blushing sunset glow
With clouds that, floating up in bridal snow,
Passed with the festal eve, rose-crowned, away?

And now, if I may trust my straining sight,
The heavens appear with added stars to-night,
And deeper depths, and more celestial height,
Than hath been reached except in dreams or death.
Hush, sweetest South! I love thy delicate breath;
But hush! methought I felt an angel's kiss!
Oh! all that lives is happy in my bliss.
That lonely fir, which always seems
As though it locked dark secrets in itself,
            Hideth a gentle elf,
Whose wand shall send me soon a frolic troop
Of rainbow visions, and of moonlit dreams.
Can joy be weary, that my eyelids droop?
To-night I shall not seek my curtained nest,
            But even here find rest.
Who whispered then? And what are they that peep
Betwixt the foliage in the tree-top there?
Come, Fairy Shadows! for the morn is near,
When to your sombre pine ye all must creep;
Come, ye wild pilots of the darkness, ere
My spirit sinks into the gulf of Sleep;
Even now it circles round and round the deep—
            ·Appear! Appear!

FLOWER-LIFE.

I think that, next to your sweet eyes,
And pleasant books, and starry skies,
    I love the world of flowers;

Less for their beauty of a day,
Than for the tender things they say,
And for a creed I've held alway,
    That they are sentient powers.

It may be matter for a smile—
And I laugh secretly the while
    I speak the fancy out—
But that they love, and that they woo,
And that they often marry too,
And do as noisier creatures do,
    I've not the faintest doubt.

And so, I cannot deem it right
To take them from the glad sunlight,
    As I have sometimes dared;
Though not without an anxious sigh
Lest this should break some gentle tie,
Some covenant of friendship, I
    Had better far have spared.

And when, in wild or thoughtless hours,
My hand hath crushed the tiniest flowers,
    I ne'er could shut from sight
The corpses of the tender things,
With other drear imaginings,
And little angel-flowers with wings
    Would haunt me through the night.

Oh! say you, friend, the creed is fraught
With sad, and even with painful thought,
    Nor could you bear to know

That such capacities belong
To creatures helpless against wrong,
At once too weak to fly the strong
　　Or front the feeblest foe ?

So be it always, then, with you ;
So be it—whether false or true—
　　I press my faith on none ;
If other fancies please you more,
The flowers shall blossom as before,
Dear as the Sibyl-leaves of yore,
　　But senseless, every one.

Yet, though I give you no reply,
It were not hard to justify
　　My creed to partial ears ;
But, conscious of the cruel part,
My rhymes would flow with faltering art,
I could not plead against your heart,
　　Nor reason with your tears.

———•———

YOUTH AND MANHOOD.

Another year ! a short one, if it flow
　　Like that just past,
And I shall stand—if years can make me so—
　　A man at last.

Yet, while the hours permit me, I would pause
　　And contemplate

The lot whereto unalterable laws
    Have bound my fate.

Yet, from the starry regions of my youth,
    The empyreal height
Where dreams are happiness, and feeling truth,
    And life delight—

From that ethereal and serene abode
    My soul would gaze
Downward upon the wide and winding road,
    Where manhood plays;

Plays with the baubles and the gauds of earth—
    Wealth, power, and fame—
Nor knows that in the twelvemonth after birth
    He did the same.

Where the descent begins, through long defiles
    I see them wind;
And some are looking down with hopeful smiles,
    And some are—blind.

And farther on a gay and glorious green
    Dazzles the sight,
While noble forms are moving o'er the scene,
    Like things of light.

Towers, temples, domes of perfect symmetry
    Rise broad and high,
With pinnacles among the clouds; ah, me!
    None touch the sky.

None pierce the pure and lofty atmosphere
  Which I breathe now,
And the strong spirits that inhabit there,
  Live—God sees how.

Sick of the very treasure which they heap;
  Their tearless eyes
Sealed ever in a heaven-forgetting sleep,
  Whose dreams are lies;

And so, a motley, unattractive throng,
  They toil and plod,
Dead to the holy ecstasies of song,
  To love, and God.

Dear God! if that I may not keep through life
  My trust, my truth,
And that I must, in yonder endless strife,
  Lose faith with youth;

If the same toil which indurates the hand
  Must steel the heart,
Till, in the wonders of the ideal land,
  It have no part;

Oh! take me hence! I would no longer stay
  Beneath the sky;
Give me to chant one pure and deathless lay,
  And let me die!

A SUMMER SHOWER.

Welcome, rain or tempest
   From yon airy powers,
We have languished for them
   Many sultry hours,
And earth is sick and wan, and pines with all her
   flowers.

What have they been doing
   In the burning June?
Riding with the genii?
   Visiting the moon?
Or sleeping on the ice amid an arctic noon?

Bring they with them jewels
   From the sunset lands?
What are these they scatter
   With such lavish hands?
There are no brighter gems in Raolconda's sands.

Pattering on the gravel,
   Dropping from the eaves,
Glancing in the grass, and
   Tinkling on the leaves,
They flash the liquid pearls as flung from fairy sieves.

Meanwhile, unreluctant,
   Earth like Danae lies;

Listen! is it fancy,
That beneath us sighs,
As that warm lap receives the largesse of the skies?

Jove, it is, descendeth
In those crystal rills;
And this world-wide tremor
Is a pulse that thrills
To a god's life infused through veins of velvet hills.

Wait, thou jealous sunshine,
Break not on their bliss;
Earth will blush in roses
Many a day for this,
And bend a brighter brow beneath thy burning kiss.

BABY'S AGE.

She came with April blooms and showers;
We count her little life by flowers.
As buds the rose upon her cheek,
We choose a flower for every week.
A week of hyacinths, we say,
And one of heart's-ease, ushered May;
And then because two wishes met
Upon the rose and violet—
I liked the Beauty, Kate, the Nun—
The violet and the rose count one.
A week the apple marked with white;
A week the lily scored in light;

Red poppies closed May's happy moon,
And tulips this blue week in June.
Here end as yet the flowery links;
To-day begins the week of pinks;
But soon—so grave, and deep, and wise
The meaning grows in Baby's eyes,
So *very* deep for Baby's age—
We think to date a week with sage!

HARK TO THE SHOUTING WIND.

Hark to the shouting Wind!
  Hark to the flying Rain!
And I care not though I never see
  A bright blue sky again.

There are thoughts in my breast to-day
  That are not for human speech;
But I hear them in the driving storm,
  And the roar upon the beach.

And oh, to be with that ship
  That I watch through the blinding brine!
O Wind! for thy sweep of land and sea!
  O Sea! for a voice like thine!

Shout on, thou pitiless Wind,
  To the frightened and flying Rain!
I care not though I never see
  A calm blue sky again.

THE MESSENGER ROSE.

If you have seen a richer glow,
Pray, tell me where your roses blow!
Look! coral-leaved! and—mark these spots!
Red staining red in crimson clots,
Like a sweet lip bitten through
In a pique.   There, where that hue
Is spilt in drops, some fairy thing
Hath gashed the azure of its wing.
Or thence, perhaps, this very morn,
Plucked the splinters of a thorn.

Rose! I make thy bliss my care!
In my lady's dusky hair
Thou shalt burn this coming night,
With even a richer crimson light.
To requite me thou shalt tell—
What I might not say as well—
How I love her; how, in brief,
On a certain crimson leaf
In my bosom, is a debt
Writ in deeper crimson yet.
If she wonder what it be—
But she'll guess it, I foresee—
Tell her that I date it, pray,
From the first sweet night in **May.**

TOO LONG, O SPIRIT OF STORM!

Too long, O Spirit of Storm,
  Thy lightning sleeps in its sheath!
I am sick to the soul of yon pallid sky,
  And the moveless sea beneath.

Come down in thy strength on the deep!
  Worse dangers there are in life,
When the waves are still, and the skies look fair,
  Than in their wildest strife.

A friend I knew, whose days
  Were as calm as this sky overhead;
But one blue morn that was fairest of all,
  The heart in his bosom fell dead.

And they thought him alive while he walked
  The streets that he walked in youth—
Ah! little they guessed the seeming man
  Was a soulless corpse in sooth.

Come down in thy strength, O Storm!
  And lash the deep till it raves!
I am sick to the soul of that quiet sea,
  Which hides ten thousand graves.

9

THE LILY CONFIDANTE.

Lily! lady of the garden!
  Let me press my lip to thine!
Love must tell its story, Lily!
  Listen thou to mine.

Two I choose to know the secret—
  Thee, and yonder wordless flute:
Dragons watch me, tender Lily,
  And thou must be mute.

There's a maiden, and her name is ....
  Hist! was that a rose-leaf fell?
See, the rose is listening, Lily,
  And the rose may tell.

Lily-browed and lily-hearted,
  She is very dear to me;
Lovely? yes, if being lovely
  Is—resembling thee.

Six to half a score of summers
  Make the sweetest of the "teens"—
Not too young to guess, dear Lily,
  What a lover means.

Laughing girl, and thoughtful woman,
  I am puzzled how to woo—
Shall I praise, or pique her, Lily?
  Tell me what to do.

" Silly lover, if thy Lily
  Like her sister lilies be,
Thou must woo, if thou wouldst wear her,
  With a simple plea.

" Love's the lover's only magic,
  Truth the very subtlest art;
Love that feigns, and lips that flatter,
  Win no modest heart.

" Like the dewdrop in my bosom,
  Be thy guileless language, youth :
Falsehood buyeth falsehood only,
  Truth must purchase truth.

" As thou talkest at the fireside,
  With the little children by—
As thou prayest in the darkness,
  When thy God is nigh—

" With a speech as chaste and gentle,
  And such meanings as become
Ear of child, or ear of angel,
  Speak, or be thou dumb.

" Woo her thus, and she shall give thee
  Of her heart the sinless whole,
All the girl within her bosom,
  And her woman's soul."

ON PRESSING SOME FLOWERS.

So, they are dead!   Love! when they passed
   From thee to me, our fingers met;
O withered darlings of the May!
   I feel those fairy fingers yet.

And for the bliss ye brought me then,
   Your faded forms are precious things;
No flowers so fair, no buds so sweet
   Shall bloom through all my future springs.

And so, pale ones! with hands as soft
   As if I closed a baby's eyes,
I'll lay you in some favorite book
   Made sacred by a poet's sighs.

Your lips shall press the sweetest song,
   The sweetest, saddest song I know,
As ye had perished, in your pride,
   Of some lone bard's melodious woe.

Oh, Love! hath love no holier shrine!
   Oh, heart! could love but lend the power,
I'd lay thy crimson pages bare,
   And every leaf should fold its flower.

A COMMON THOUGHT.

Somewhere on this earthly planet
   In the dust of flowers to be,
In the dewdrop, in the sunshine,
   Sleeps a solemn day for me.

At this wakeful hour of midnight
   I behold it dawn in mist,
And I hear a sound of sobbing
   Through the darkness—hist! oh, hist!

In a dim and musky chamber,
   I am breathing life away;
Some one draws a curtain softly,
   And I watch the broadening day.

As it purples in the zenith,
   As it brightens on the lawn,
There's a hush of death about me,
   And a whisper, " He is gone!"

SONNET.

Poet! if on a lasting fame be bent
Thy unperturbing hopes, thou wilt not roam
Too far from thine own happy heart and home;
Cling to the lowly earth, and be content!
So shall thy name be dear to many a heart;
So shall the noblest truths by thee be taught;

The flower and fruit of wholesome human thought
Bless the sweet labors of thy gentle art.
The brightest stars are nearest to the earth,
And we may track the mighty sun above,
Even by the shadow of a slender flower.
Always, O bard, humility is power!
And thou may'st draw from matters of the hearth
Truths wide as nations, and as deep as love.

SONNET.

Most men know love but as a part of life;
They hide it in some corner of the breast,
Even from themselves; and only when they rest
In the brief pauses of that daily strife,
Wherewith the world might else be not so rife,
They draw it forth (as one draws forth a toy
To soothe some ardent, kiss-exacting boy)
And hold it up to sister, child, or wife.
Ah me! why may not love and life be one?
Why walk we thus alone, when by our side,
Love, like a visible God, might be our guide?
How would the marts grow noble! and the street,
Worn like a dungeon-floor by weary feet,
Seem then a golden court-way of the Sun!

SONNET.

Life ever seems as from its present site
It aimed to lure us.   Mountains of the past
It melts, with all their crags and caverns vast,
Into a purple cloud !   Across the night
Which hides what is to be, it shoots a light
All rosy with the yet unrisen dawn.
Not the near daisies, but yon distant height
Attracts us, lying on this emerald lawn.
And always, be the landscape what it may—
Blue, misty hill or sweep of glimmering plain—
It is the eye's endeavor still to gain
The fine, faint limit of the bounding day.
God, haply, in this mystic mode, would fain
Hint of a happier home, far, far away !

SONNET.

They dub thee idler, smiling sneeringly,
And why ? because, forsooth, so many moons,
Here dwelling voiceless by the voiceful sea,
Thou hast not set thy thoughts to paltry tunes
In song or sonnet.   Them these golden noons
Oppress not with their beauty ; they could prate,
Even while a prophet read the solemn runes
On which is hanging some imperial fate.
How know they, these good gossips, what to thee
The ocean and its wanderers may have brought ?

How know they, in their busy vacancy,
With what far aim thy spirit may be fraught?
Or that thou dost not bow thee silently
Before some great unutterable thought?

SONNET.

Some truths there be are better left unsaid;
Much is there that we may not speak unblamed.
On words, as wings, how many joys have fled!
The jealous fairies love not to be named.
There is an old-world tale of one whose bed
A genius graced, to all, save him, unknown;
One day the secret passed his lips, and sped
As secrets speed—thenceforth he slept alone.
Too much, oh! far too much is told in books;
Too broad a daylight wraps us all and each.
Ah! it is well that, deeper than our looks,
Some secrets lie beyond conjecture's reach.
Ah! it is well that in the soul are nooks
That will not open to the keys of speech.

SONNET.

I scarcely grieve, O Nature! at the lot
That pent my life within a city's bounds,
And shut me from thy sweetest sights and sounds.
Perhaps I had not learned, if some lone cot

Had nursed a dreamy childhood, what the mart
Taught me amid its turmoil; so my youth
Had missed full many a stern but wholesome truth.
Here, too, O Nature! in this haunt of Art,
Thy power is on me, and I own thy thrall.
There is no unimpressive spot on earth!
The beauty of the stars is over all,
And Day and Darkness visit every hearth.
Clouds do not scorn us: yonder factory's smoke
Looked like a golden mist when morning broke.

SONNET.

Grief dies like joy; the tears upon my cheek
Will disappear like dew. Dear God! I know
Thy kindly Providence hath made it so,
And thank thee for the law. I am too weak
To make a friend of Sorrow, or to wear,
With that dark angel ever by my side
(Though to thy heaven there be no better guide),
A front of manly calm. Yet, for I hear
How woe hath cleansed, how grief can deify,
So weak a thing it seems that grief should die,
And love and friendship with it, I could pray,
That if it might not gloom upon my brow,
Nor weigh upon my arm as it doth now,
No grief of mine should ever pass away.

SONNET.

At last, beloved Nature! I have met
Thee face to face upon thy breezy hills,
And boldly, where thy inmost bowers are set,
Gazed on thee naked in thy mountain rills.
When first I felt thy breath upon my brow.
Tears of strange ecstasy gushed out like rain,
And with a longing, passionate as vain,
I strove to clasp thee.   But, I know not how,
Always before me didst thou seem to glide ;
And often from one sunny mountain-side,
Upon the next bright peak I saw thee kneel,
And heard thy voice upon the billowy blast ;
But, climbing, only reached that shrine to feel
The shadow of a Presence which had passed.

SONNET.

I know not why, but all this weary day,
Suggested by no definite grief or pain,
Sad fancies have been flitting through my brain ;
Now it has been a vessel losing way,
Rounding a stormy headland ; now a gray
Dull waste of clouds above a wintry main ;
And then, a banner, drooping in the rain,
And meadows beaten into bloody clay.
Strolling at random with this shadowy woe
At heart, I chanced to wander hither!   Lo!

A league of desolate marsh-land, with its lush,
Hot grasses in a noisome, tide-left bed,
And faint, warm airs, that rustle in the hush,
Like whispers round the body of the dead!

———•———

SONNET.

(WRITTEN ON A VERY SMALL SHEET OF NOTE-PAPER.)

Were I the poet-laureate of the fairies,
Who in a rose-leaf finds too broad a page ;
Or could I, like your beautiful canaries,
Sing with free heart and happy, in a cage ;
Perhaps I might within this little space
(As in some Eastern tale, by magic power,
A giant is imprisoned in a flower)
Have told you something with a poet's grace.
But I need wider limits, ampler scope,
A world of freedom for a world of passion,
And even then, the glory of my hope
Would not be uttered in its stateliest fashion ;
Yet, lady, when fit language shall have told it,
You'll find one little heart enough to hold it!

1866.

ADDRESSED TO THE OLD YEAR.

Art thou not glad to close
  Thy wearied eyes, O saddest child of Time,
  Eyes which have looked on every mortal crime,
And swept the piteous round of mortal woes ?

In dark Plutonian caves,
  Beneath the lowest deep, go, hide thy head ;
  Or earth thee where the blood that thou hast shed
May trickle on thee from thy countless graves !

Take with thee all thy gloom
  And guilt, and all our griefs, save what the breast,
  Without a wrong to some dear shadowy guest,
May not surrender even to the tomb.

No tear shall weep thy fall,
  When, as the midnight bell doth toll thy fate,
  Another lifts the sceptre of thy state,
And sits a monarch in thine ancient hall.

Him all the hours attend,
  With a new hope like morning in their eyes ;
  Him the fair earth and him these radiant skies
Hail as their sovereign, welcome as their friend.

Him, too, the nations wait ;
  " O lead us from the shadow of the Past,"

In a long wail like this December blast,
They cry, and, crying, grow less desolate.

How he will shape his sway
    They ask not—for old doubts and fears will cling—
    And yet they trust that, somehow, he will bring
A sweeter sunshine than thy mildest day.

Beneath his gentle hand
    They hope to see no meadow, vale, or hill
    Stained with a deeper red than roses spill,
When some too boisterous zephyr sweeps the land.

A time of peaceful prayer,
    Of law, love, labor, honest loss and gain—
    These are the visions of the coming reign
Now floating to them on this wintry air.

ADDITIONAL POEMS.

ODE.

SUNG ON THE OCCASION OF DECORATING THE GRAVES
OF THE CONFEDERATE DEAD, AT MAGNOLIA CEME-
TERY, CHARLESTON, S. C., 1867.

I.

Sleep sweetly in your humble graves,
    Sleep, martyrs of a fallen cause;
Though yet no marble column craves
    The pilgrim here to pause.

II.

In seeds of laurel in the earth
    The blossom of your fame is blown,
And somewhere, waiting for its birth,
    The shaft is in the stone!

III.

Meanwhile, behalf the tardy years
    Which keep in trust your storied tombs,
Behold! your sisters bring their tears,
    And these memorial blooms.

IV.

Small tributes! but your shades will smile
    More proudly on these wreaths to-day,
Than when some cannon-moulded pile
    Shall overlook this bay.

V.

Stoop, angels, hither from the skies!
　　There is no holier spot of ground
Than where defeated valor lies,
　　By mourning beauty crowned!

————◆————

HYMN.

SUNG AT A SACRED CONCERT AT COLUMBIA, S. C.

I.

Faint falls the gentle voice of prayer
In the wild sounds that fill the air,
Yet, Lord, we know that voice is heard,
Not less than if Thy throne it stirred.

II.

Thine ear, thou tender One, is caught,
If we but bend the knee in thought;
No choral song that shakes the sky
Floats farther than the Christian's sigh.

III.

Not all the darkness of the land
Can hide the lifted eye and hand;
Nor need the clanging conflict cease,
To make Thee hear our cries for peace.

THE STREAM IS FLOWING FROM THE WEST.

The stream is flowing from the west;
    As if it poured from yonder skies,
It wears upon its rippling breast
    The sunset's golden dyes;
And bearing onward to the sea,
'Twill clasp the isle that holdeth thee.

I dip my hand within the wave;
    Ah! how impressionless and cold!
I touch it with my lip, and lave
    My forehead in the gold.
It is a trivial thought, but sweet,
Perhaps the wave will kiss thy feet.

Alas! I leave no trace behind—
    As little on the senseless stream
As on thy heart, or on thy mind;
    Which was the simpler dream,
To win that warm, wild love of thine,
Or make the water whisper mine?

Dear stream! some moons must wax and wane
    Ere I again shall cross thy tide,
And then, perhaps, a viewless chain
    Will drag me to her side,
To love with all my spirit's scope,
To wish, do everything but—hope.

STANZAS.

A MOTHER GAZES UPON HER DAUGHTER, ARRAYED
FOR AN APPROACHING BRIDAL.   WRITTEN IN IL-
LUSTRATION OF A TABLEAU VIVANT.

Is she not lovely!   Oh! when, long ago,
  My own dead mother gazed upon my face,
As I stood blushing near in bridal snow,
  I had not half her beauty and her grace.

Yet that fond mother praised, the world caressed,
  And *one* adored me—how shall *he* who soon
Shall wear my gentle flower upon his breast,
  Prize to its utmost worth the priceless boon?

Shall he not gird her, guard her, make her rich,
  (Not as the world is rich, in outward show,)
With all the love and watchful kindness which
  A wise and tender manhood may bestow?

Oh! I shall part from her with many tears,
  My earthly treasure, pure and undefiled!
And not without a weight of anxious fears
  For the new future of my darling child.

And yet—for well I know that virgin heart—
  No wifely duty will she leave undone;
Nor will her love neglect that woman's art
  Which courts and keeps a love already won.

In no light girlish levity she goes
   Unto the altar where they wait her now,
But with a thoughtful, prayerful heart that knows
   The solemn purport of a marriage vow.

And she will keep, with all her soul's deep truth,
   The lightest pledge which binds her love and life;
And she will be—no less in age than youth
   My noble child will be—a noble wife.

And he, her lover! husband! what of him?
   Yes, he will shield, I think, my bud from blight!
Yet griefs will come—enough! my eyes are dim
   With tears I must not shed—at least, to-night.

Bless thee, my daughter!—Oh! she is so fair!—
   Heaven bend above thee with its starriest skies!
And make thee truly all thou dost appear
   Unto a lover's and thy mother's eyes!

RETIREMENT.

My gentle friend! I hold no creed so false
As that which dares to teach that we are born
For battle only, and that in this life
The soul, if it would burn with starlike power,
Must needs forsooth be kindled by the sparks
Struck from the shock of clashing human hearts.

There is a wisdom that grows up in strife,
And one—I like it best—that sits at home
And learns its lessons of a thoughtful ease.
So come! a lonely house awaits thee!—there
Nor praise, nor blame shall reach us, save what love
Of knowledge for itself shall wake at times
In our own bosoms; come! and we will build
A wall of quiet thought, and gentle books,
Betwixt us and the hard and bitter world.
Sometimes—for we need not be anchorites—
A distant friend shall cheer us through the Post,
Or some Gazette—of course no partisan—
Shall bring us pleasant news of pleasant things;
Then, twisted into graceful allumettes,
Each ancient joke shall blaze with genuine flame
To light our pipes and candles; but to wars,
Whether of words or weapons, we shall be
Deaf—so we twain shall pass away the time
Ev'n as a pair of happy lovers, who,
Alone, within some quiet garden-nook,
With a clear night of stars above their heads,
Just hear, betwixt their kisses and their talk,
The tumult of a tempest rolling through
A chain of neighboring mountains; they awhile
Pause to admire a flash that only shows
The smile upon their faces, but, full soon,
Turn with a quick, glad impulse, and perhaps
A conscious wile that brings them closer yet,
To dally with their own fond hearts, and play
With the sweet flowers that blossom at their feet.

VOX ET PRETEREA NIHIL.

I've been haunted all night, I've been haunted all day,
By the ghost of a song, by the shade of a lay,
That with meaningless words and profusion of rhyme,
To a dreamy and musical rhythm keeps time.
A simple, but still a most magical strain,
Its dim monotones have bewildered my brain
With a specious and cunning appearance of thought,
I seem to be catching but never have caught.

I know it embodies some very sweet things,
And can almost divine the low burden it sings;
But again, and again, and still ever again,
It has died on my ear at the touch of my pen.
And so it keeps courting and shunning my quest,
As a bird that has just been aroused from her nest,
Too fond to depart, and too frightened to stay,
Now circles about you, now flutters away.

Oh! give me fit words for that exquisite song,
And thou could'st not, proud beauty! be obdurate long;
It would come like the voice of a saint from above,
And win thee to kindness, and melt thee to love.
Not gilded with fancy, nor frigid with art,
But simple as feeling, and warm as the heart,
It would murmur my name with so charming a tone,
As would almost persuade thee to wish it thine own.

HYMN.

SUNG AT AN ANNIVERSARY OF THE ASYLUM OF
ORPHANS AT CHARLESTON.

We scarce, O God! could lisp thy name,
  When those who loved us passed away,
And left us but thy love to claim,
  With but an infant's strength to pray.

Thou gav'st that Refuge and that Shrine,
  At which we learn to know thy ways;
Father! the fatherless are thine!
  Thou wilt not spurn the orphan's praise.

Yet hear a single cry of pain!
  Lord! whilst we dream in quiet beds,
The summer sun and winter rain
  Beat still on many homeless heads.

And o'er this weary earth, we know,
  Young outcasts roam the waste and wave;
And little hands are clasped in woe
  Above some tender mother's grave.

Ye winds! keep every storm aloof,
  And kiss away the tears they weep!
Ye skies, that make their only roof,
  Look gently on their houseless sleep!

And thou, O Friend and Father! find
  A home to shield their helpless youth!
Dear hearts to love—sweet ties to bind—
  And guide and guard them in the truth!

———◆———

TO A CAPTIVE OWL.

I should be dumb before thee, feathered sage!
  And gaze upon thy phiz with solemn awe,
But for a most audacious wish to gauge
  The hoarded wisdom of thy learned craw.

Art thou, grave bird! so wondrous wise indeed?
  Speak freely, without fear of jest or jibe—
What is thy moral and religious creed?
  And what the metaphysics of thy tribe?

A Poet, curious in birds and brutes,
  I do not question thee in idle play;
What is thy station? What are thy pursuits?
  Doubtless thou hast thy pleasures—what are *they?*

Or is't thy wont to muse and mouse at once,
  Entice thy prey with airs of meditation,
And with the unvarying habits of a dunce,
  To dine in solemn depths of contemplation?

10

There may be much—the world at least says so—
  Behind that ponderous brow and thoughtful gaze;
Yet such a great philosopher should know,
  It is by no means wise to think always.

And, Bird, despite thy meditative air,
  I hold thy stock of wit but paltry pelf—
Thou show'st that same grave aspect everywhere,
  And wouldst look thoughtful, stuffed, upon a shelf.

I grieve to be so plain, renownëd Bird—
  Thy fame's a flam, and thou an empty fowl;
And what is more, upon a Poet's word
  I'd say as much, wert thou Minerva's owl.

So doff th' imposture of those heavy brows;
  They do not serve to hide thy instincts base—
And if thou must be sometimes munching *mouse,*
  Munch it, O Owl! with less profound a face.

———◆———

LOVE'S LOGIC.

And if I ask thee for a kiss,
  I ask no more than this sweet breeze,
With far less title to the bliss,
  Steals every minute at his ease.

And yet how placid is thy brow!
  It seems to woo the bold caress,
While now he takes his kiss, and now
  All sorts of freedoms with thy dress.

Or if I dare thy hand to touch,
  Hath nothing pressed its palm before?
A flower, I'm sure, hath done as much,
  And ah! some senseless diamond more.
It strikes me, love, the very rings,
  Now sparkling on that hand of thine,
Could tell some truly startling things,
  If they had tongues or touch like mine.

Indeed, indeed, I do not know
  Of all that thou hast power to grant,
A boon for which I could not show
  Some pretty precedent extant.
Suppose, for instance, I should clasp
  Thus,—so,—and thus!—thy slender waist—
I would not hold within my grasp
  More than this loosened zone embraced.

Oh! put the anger from thine eyes,
  Or shut them if they still must frown;
Those lids, despite yon garish skies,
  Can bring a timely darkness down.
Then, if in that convenient night,
  My lips should press thy dewy mouth,
The touch shall be so soft, so light,
  Thou'lt fancy me—this gentle South.

SECOND LOVE.

Could I reveal the secret joy
   Thy presence always with it brings,
The memories so strangely waked
   Of long forgotten things,

The love, the hope, the fear, the grief,
   Which with that voice come back to me,—
Thou wouldst forgive the impassioned gaze
   So often turned on thee.

It was, indeed, that early love,
   But foretaste of this second one,—
The soft light of the morning star
   Before the morning sun.

The same dark beauty in her eyes,
   The same blonde hair and placid brow,
The same deep-meaning, quiet smile
   Thou bendest on me now,

She might have been, she *was* no more
   Than what a prescient hope could make,—
A dear presentiment of thee
   I loved but for thy sake.

HYMN.

SUNG AT THE CONSECRATION OF MAGNOLIA CEMETERY, CHARLESTON, S. C.

Whose was the hand that painted thee, O Death!
In the false aspect of a ruthless foe,
Despair and sorrow waiting on thy breath—
O gentle Power! who could have wronged thee so?

Thou rather should'st be crowned with fadeless flowers,
Of lasting fragrance and celestial hue;
Or be thy couch amid funereal bowers,
But let the stars and sunlight sparkle through.

So, with these thoughts before us, we have fixed
And beautified, O Death! thy mansion here,
Where gloom and gladness—grave and garden—mixed,
Make it a place to love, and not to fear.

Heaven! shed thy most propitious dews around!
Ye holy stars! look down with tender eyes,
And gild and guard, and consecrate the ground
Where we may rest, and whence we pray to rise.

LINES TO R. L.

That which we are and shall be is made up
Of what we have been.   On the autumn leaf
The crimson stains bear witness of its spring;

And, on its perfect nodes, the ocean shell
Notches the slow, strange changes of its growth.
Ourselves are our own records ; if we looked
Rightly into that blotted crimson page
Within our bosoms, then there were no need
To chronicle our stories ; for the heart
Hath, like the earth, its strata, and contains
Its past within its present.   Well for us,
And our most cherished secrets, that within
The round of being few there are who read
Beneath the surface.   Else our very forms,
The merest gesture of our hands, might tell
Much we would hide forever.   Know you not
Those eyes, in whose dark heaven I have gazed
More curiously than on my favorite stars,
Are deeper for such griefs as they have seen,
And brighter for the fancies they have shrined,
And sweeter for the loves which they have talked ?
Oh ! that I had the power to read their smiles,
Or sound the depth of all their glorious gloom.
So should I learn your history from its birth,
Through all its glad and grave experiences,
Better than if—(your journal in my hand,
Written as only women write, with all
A woman's shades and shapes of feeling, traced
As with the fine touch of a needle's point)—
I followed you from that bright hour when first
I saw you in the garden 'mid the flowers,
To that wherein a letter from your hand
Made me all rich with the dear name of friend.

MADELINE.

O lady! if, until this hour,
　I've gazed in those bewildering eyes,
Yet never owned their touching power,
　But when thou could'st not hear my sighs;
It has not been that love has slept
　One single moment in my soul,
Or that on lip or look I kept
　A stern and stoical control;
But that I saw, but that I felt,
　In every tone and glance of thine,
Whate'er they spoke, where'er they dwelt,
　How small, how poor a part was mine;
And that I deeply, dearly knew,
　That hidden, hopeless love confessed,
The fatal words would lose me, too,
　Even the weak friendship I possessed.

And so, I masked my secret well;
　The very love within my breast
Became the strange, but potent spell
　By which I forced it into rest.
Yet there were times—I scarce know how
　These eager lips refrained to speak,—
Some kindly smile would light thy brow,
　And I grew passionate and weak;
The secret sparkled at my eyes,
And love but half repressed its sighs,—
Then had I gazed an instant more,

Or dwelt one moment on that brow,
I might have changed the smile it wore,
    To what perhaps it weareth now,
And spite of all I feared to meet,
Confessed that passion at thy feet.
To save my heart, to spare thine own,
    There was one remedy alone.
I fled, I shunned thy very touch,—
It cost me much, O God! how much!
But if some burning tears were shed,
    Lady! I let them freely flow;
At least, they left unbreathed, unsaid,
    A worse and wilder woe.

But now,—*now* that we part indeed,
    And that I may not think as then,
That as I wish, or as I need,
    I may return again,—
Now that for months, perhaps for years—
I see no limit in my fears—
My home shall be some distant spot,
Where thou—where even thy name is not,
And since I shall not see the frown,
Such wild, mad language must bring down,
Could I—albeit I may not sue
    In hope to bend thy steadfast will—
Could I have breathed this word, adieu,
    And kept my secret still?

Doubtless thou know'st the Hebrew story—
    The tale's with me a favorite one—

How Raphael left the Courts of Glory,
    And walked with Judah's honored Son;
And how the twain together dwelt,
    And how they talked upon the road,
How often too they must have knelt
    As equals to the same kind God;
And still the mortal never guessed,
How much and deeply he was blessed,
Till when—the Angel's mission done—
    The spell which drew him earthwards, riven—
The lover saved—the maiden won—
    He plumed again his wings for Heaven;
O Madeline! as unaware
Thou hast been followed everywhere,
    And girt and guarded by a love,
As warm, as tender in its care,
As pure, ay, powerful in prayer,
    As any saint above!
Like the bright inmate of the skies,
It only looked with friendly eyes,
And still had worn the illusive guise,
    And thus at least been half concealed;
But at this parting, painful hour,
It spreads its wings, unfolds its power,
    And stands, like Raphael, revealed.

More, Lady! I would wish to speak,—
But it were vain, and words are weak,
And now that I have bared my breast,
Perchance thou wilt infer the rest.
So, so, farewell! I need not say

10*

I look, I ask for no reply,
The cold and scarcely pitying "nay"
   I read in that unmelted eye;
Yet one dear favor, let me pray!
   Days, months, however slow to me,
Must drag at last their length away,
   And I return—if not to thee—
At least to breathe the same sweet air
That woos thy lips and waves thy hair.
Oh, then!—these daring lines forgot—
Look, speak, as thou hadst read them not.
So, Lady, may I still retain
A right I would not lose again,
For all that gold or guilt can buy,
Or all that Heaven itself deny,
A right such love may justly claim,
Of seeing thee in friendship's name.
Give me but this, and still at whiles,
A portion of thy faintest smiles,
   It were enough to bless;
I may not, dare not ask for more
Than boon so rich, and yet so poor,
   But I should die with less.

TO WHOM?

Awake upon a couch of pain,
   I see a star betwixt the trees;
Across yon darkening field of cane,
   Comes slow and soft the evening breeze.
My curtain's folds are faintly stirred;
   And moving lightly in her rest,
I hear the chirrup of a bird,
   That dreameth in some neighboring nest.

Last night I took no note of these—
   How it was passed I scarce can say;
'Twas not in prayers to Heaven for ease,
   'Twas not in wishes for the day.
Impatient tears, and passionate sighs,
   Touched as with fire the pulse of pain,—
I cursed, and cursed the wildering eyes
   That burned this fever in my brain.

Oh! blessings on the quiet hour!
   My thoughts in calmer current flow;
She is not conscious of her power,
   And hath no knowledge of my woe.
Perhaps, if like yon peaceful star,
   She looked upon my burning brow,
She would not pity from afar,
   But kiss me as the breeze does now.

TO THEE.

Draw close the lattice and the door!
  Shut out the very stars above!
No other eyes than mine shall pore
  Upon this thrilling tale of love.
As, since the book was open last,
  Along its dear and sacred text
No other eyes than thine have passed—
  Be mine the eyes that trace it next!

Oh! very nobly is it wrought,—
  This web of love's divinest light,—
But not to feed my soul with thought,
  Hang I upon the book to-night;
I read it only for thy sake,
  To every page my lips I press—
The very leaves appear to make
  A silken rustle like thy dress.

And so, as each blest page I turn,
  I seem, with many a secret thrill,
To touch a soft white hand, and burn
  To clasp and kiss it at my will.
Oh! if a fancy be so sweet
  These shadowy fingers touching mine—
How wildly would my pulses beat,
  If they *could* feel the beat of thine!

STORM AND CALM.

Sweet are these kisses of the South,
As dropped from woman's rosiest mouth,
And tenderer are those azure skies
Than this world's tenderest pair of eyes!

But ah! beneath such influence
Thought is too often lost in Sense;
And Action, faltering as we thrill,
Sinks in the unnerved arms of Will.

Awake, thou stormy North, and blast
The subtle spells around us cast;
Beat from our limbs these flowery chains
With the sharp scourges of thy rains!

Bring with thee from thy Polar cave
All the wild songs of wind and wave,
Of toppling berg and grinding floe,
And the dread avalanche of snow!

Wrap us in Arctic night and clouds!
Yell like a fiend amid the shrouds
Of some slow-sinking vessel, when
He hears the shrieks of drowning men!

Blend in thy mighty voice whate'er
Of danger, terror, and despair
Thou hast encountered in thy sweep
Across the land and o'er the deep.

Pour in our ears all notes of woe
That, as these very moments flow,
Rise like a harsh discordant psalm,
While we lie here in tropic calm.

Sting our weak hearts with bitter shame,
Bear us along with thee like flame;
And prove that even to destroy
More God-like may be than to toy
And rust or rot in idle joy!

SONNET.

Which are the clouds, and which the mountains? See,
They mix and melt together! Yon blue hill
Looks fleeting as the vapors which distil
Their dews upon its summit, while the free
And far-off clouds, now solid, dark, and still,
An aspect wear of calm eternity.
Each seems the other, as our fancies will—
The cloud a mount, the mount a cloud, and we
Gaze doubtfully. So everywhere on earth,
This foothold where we stand with slipping feet,
The unsubstantial and substantial meet,
And we are fooled until made wise by Time.
Is not the obvious lesson something worth,
Lady? or have I wov'n an idle rhyme?

SONNET.

What gossamer lures thee now ?   What hope, what
    name
Is on thy lips ?   What dreams to fruit have grown ?
Thou who hast turned *one* Poet-heart to stone,
Is thine yet burning with its seraph flame?
Let me give back a warning of thine own,
That, falling from thee many moons ago,
Sank on my soul like the prophetic moan
Of some young Sibyl shadowing her own woe.
The words are thine, and will not do thee wrong,
I only bind their solemn charge to song.
Thy tread is on a quicksand—oh ! be wise!
Nor, in the passionate eagerness of youth,
Mistake thy bosom-serpent's glittering eyes
For the calm lights of Reason and of Truth.

SONNET.

I thank you, kind and best beloved friend,
With the same thanks one murmurs to a sister,
When, for some gentle favor, he hath kissed her,
Less for the gifts than for the love you send,
Less for the flowers, than what the flowers convey,
If I, indeed, divine their meaning truly,
And not unto myself ascribe, unduly,

Things which you neither meant nor wished to say.
Oh! tell me, is the hope then all misplaced?
And am I flattered by my own affection?
But in your beauteous gift, methought I traced
Something above a short-lived predilection,
And which, for that I know no dearer name,
I designate as love, without love's flame.

——•——

SONNET.

Are these wild thoughts, thus fettered in my rhymes,
Indeed the product of my heart and brain?
How strange that on my ear the rhythmic strain
Falls like faint memories of far-off times!
When did I feel the sorrow, act the part,
Which I have striv'n to shadow forth in song?
In what dead century swept that mingled throng
Of mighty pains and pleasures through my heart?
Not in the yesterdays of that still life
Which I have passed so free and far from strife,
But somewhere in this weary world I know,
In some strange land, beneath some orient clime,
I saw or shared a martyrdom sublime,
And felt a deeper grief than any later woe.

The Romantic Tradition in American Literature

An Arno Press Collection

Alcott, A. Bronson, editor. **Conversations with Children on the Gospels.** Boston, 1836/1837. Two volumes in one.

Bartol, C[yrus] A. **Discourses on the Christian Spirit and Life.** 2nd edition. Boston, 1850.

Boker, George H[enry]. **Poems of the War.** Boston, 1864.

Brooks, Charles T. **Poems, Original and Translated.** Selected and edited by W. P. Andrews. Boston, 1885.

Brownell, Henry Howard. **War-Lyrics** and Other Poems. Boston, 1866.

Brownson, O[restes] A. **Essays and Reviews Chiefly on Theology, Politics, and Socialism.** New York, 1852.

Channing, [William] Ellery (The Younger). **Poems.** Boston, 1843.

Channing, [William] Ellery (The Younger). **Poems of Sixty-Five Years.** Edited by F. B. Sanborn. Philadelphia and Concord, 1902.

Chivers, Thomas Holley. **Eonchs of Ruby:** A Gift of Love. New York, 1851.

Chivers, Thomas Holley. **Virginalia;** or, Songs of My Summer Nights. (Reprinted from *Research Classics,* No. 2, 1942). Philadelphia, 1853.

Cooke, Philip Pendleton. **Froissart Ballads,** and Other Poems. Philadelphia, 1847.

Cranch, Christopher Pearse. **The Bird and the Bell,** with Other Poems. Boston, 1875.

[Dall], Caroline W. Healey, editor. **Margaret and Her Friends.** Boston, 1895.

[D'Arusmont], Frances Wright. **A Few Days in Athens.** Boston, 1850.

Everett, Edward. **Orations and Speeches,** on Various Occasions. Boston, 1836.

Holland, J[osiah] G[ilbert]. **The Marble Prophecy,** and Other Poems. New York, 1872.

Huntington, William Reed. **Sonnets and a Dream.** Jamaica, N. Y., 1899.

Jackson, Helen [Hunt]. **Poems.** Boston, 1892.

Miller, Joaquin (Cincinnatus Hiner Miller). **The Complete Poetical Works of Joaquin Miller.** San Francisco, 1897.

Parker, Theodore. **A Discourse of Matters Pertaining to Religion.** Boston, 1842.

Pinkney, Edward C. **Poems.** Baltimore, 1838.

Reed, Sampson. **Observations on the Growth of the Mind.** *Including,* **Genius** (Reprinted from *Aesthetic Papers,* Boston, 1849). 5th edition. Boston, 1859.

Sill, Edward Rowland. **The Poetical Works of Edward Rowland Sill.** Boston and New York, 1906.

Simms, William Gilmore. **Poems:** Descriptive, Dramatic, Legendary and Contemplative. New York, 1853. Two volumes in one.

Simms, William Gilmore, editor. **War Poetry of the South.** New York, 1866.

Stickney, Trumbull. **The Poems of Trumbull Stickney.** Boston and New York, 1905.

Timrod, Henry. **The Poems of Henry Timrod.** Edited by Paul H. Hayne. New York, 1873.

Trowbridge, John Townsend. **The Poetical Works of John Townsend Trowbridge.** Boston and New York, 1903.

Very, Jones. **Essays and Poems.** [Edited by R. W. Emerson]. Boston, 1839.

Very, Jones. **Poems and Essays.** Boston and New York, 1886.

White, Richard Grant, editor. **Poetry:** Lyrical, Narrative, and Satirical of the Civil War. New York, 1866.

Wilde, Richard Henry. **Hesperia:** A Poem. Edited by His Son (William Wilde). Boston, 1867.

Willis, Nathaniel Parker. **The Poems, Sacred, Passionate, and Humorous, of Nathaniel Parker Willis.** New York, 1868.